Original Cartoons: The Frederator Studios Postcards 1998-2005

Edited by
Eric Homan & Fred Seibert

Frederator logo designed by Adams-Morioka, Los Angeles.

Electronic graphics production by Kenny Peers.

Print production by Barry Friedland and Melinda Fry at InnerWorkings.

Cover illustration by Craig Kellman.

ISBN 0-9743806-3-6

First Frederator Books printing 2005

www.frederator.kz

Printed in Canada.

Acknowledgements, FS

My first take on these appreciations ran for five pages, and didn't come close to expressing exactly how important these people were to the contents of this book. So, please forgive the brevity, the seemingly cavalier sameness of each entry, and to all those I've inadvertantly left off.

Thank you to all the creators, writers, and artists.

And thank you to Sean Adams, Joe Barbera, Debby Beece, Marc Chamlin, Carlton Clay, Margie Cohn, William Dunnigan, Tom Freston, Mike Glenn, Emily Gmerek-Hache, Alan Goodman, Bill Hanna, Albie Hecht, Debby Hindman, Larry Huber, Alex Kamnitsis, Alan Kaufman, Richard Koenigsberg, John Kricfalusi, Roy Langbord, Judy McGrath, Brian Miller, Noreen Morioka, Susie Norris-Epstein, Travis Pomposello, Dale Pon, Jennifer Powell, Emil Rensing, Scott Sassa, Herb Scannell, Jim Scott, Jed Simmons, Anne Sweeney, Mark Taylor, Scott Webb, Cyma Zarghami.

Thank you to my co-editor Eric Homan.

My mother Lilliana and father George never said no to my interests, curiosities and passions.

My family – Robin, and my sons Jack and Joe – inspire, support, and love unconditionally, and let me go wherever I go. Thank you can't be enough.

Contents

Preface

In 1998, thirty-four mavericks gathered in the armpit of North Hollywood, California, to create original cartoons for the kids of America. With only their unique visions, a lifetime of talent, and piles of pencils and paper, they set out against the grain of the mainstream animation business so they could make some really funny hits.

They've become the new world-class talents.

We all started making original cartoons at the Hanna-Barbera studios in the early 1990s. And consciously or not we wanted to stage a coup. An upsetting of a world where 'animation' had replaced cartoons, where 'family entertainment' had replaced kids' TV, where 'role models' had replaced the just plain funny characters we all remembered. Our rogues went 'back to the future' in the way cartoons are conceived and produced and have spawned lots of big hits. However, I think it's fair to say that every one of the 100 shorts are not only lavishly designed and outrageously funny but also deeply personal, conceived by individualistic filmmakers with voices and skills equal to any of the greatest movie comedians in the history of cinema.

The postcards (and posters) in this book are also part of our attempt to bring attention to the indisputable gifts of our team. There was a day when a cartoon short in a movie theatre was accompanied by its own one sheet poster or lobby card. All along our intention has been to highlight each and every one of our creators and characters, to make the film world aware of the exceptional in our medium.

Of course, the outpouring of positive response to our cards led us to be completely full of ourselves, and before you knew it we felt empty if we weren't mailing something out, even when we were out of production. So you get a little something to remind folks about Frederator Studios with some harmless fun and hopeless sentimentality. So far that's meant five series of postcards and other assorted posters. We thought that collecting them in this book would save us from dozens of boxes of printed matter cluttering the office. Actually, all it's done is give us more work we enjoy, and added thousands more pieces of paper on our shelves.

In the end, all of us at the studio are just big fans. These postcards remind us of the fantastic talent that has agreed to be part of our club. Thanks all, the world is a funnier place with you around.

Fred Seibert
New York 2005

Fred Seibert founded Frederator Studios in 1998 after five years as president of Hanna-Barbera Cartoons. He is the Executive Producer of six cartoon series on Nickelodeon.

Foreward

Spare Me Your Chrome And Linen

My name is Eric H. and I'm a deltiologist.

Whew. I feel better already.

I got my first taste of collecting postcards way back in 2000 when I snagged a smart turn-of-the-last-century card showing Manhattan's commodious Wanamaker building, a building I was working in at the time. Well, this card led to another, these cards led to others, and so on. That's the way it happens.

I kept my new-found mania kind of quiet for a while, thinking that being labeled 'deltiologist' would conflict with the brand of cool I had cultivated since junior high school. There was My Public to consider.

However, I recently decided to come clean while browsing through boxes of ephemera at the Pasadena Elks Hall during a paper collectibles sale. As I sorted and rummaged, I wondered (out loud, of course – conversing with one's self is encouraged among the faithful) why a guy like me took this path. Besides the pathological compulsiveness, of course. Presented with the opportunity to create a list, I came up with three factors which motivate me to collect postcards (the world's third-largest collectible hobby, I might add): the practical; the historical; and the aesthetic.

It may come as a surprise, but postcards of a century ago were actually used to communicate real *information*. Information relating to the humidity in Poughkeepsie and the status of Cousin Eli's croup, for instance. None of this "Having a lovely time - Wish you were here!" banality. It's like the difference of honking your horn in a traffic jam (practical) versus honking your horn to the beat of whatever song your listening to (impractical, but fun). Function over form, that's my motto.

Besides the social history (real life is made of humidity and croup) there's the other kind of history (anti-social?) as well. To get a glimpse of Main Street in 1902 Palmer, Massachusetts, or New Orleans' Royal Street's long-gone trolley tracks is to get a glimpse of who we are as a people. (I'm not sure what that means, but I've heard Ken Burns say it about everything from the Civil War to Huey Long. And he's very smart.)

And what can be said about the art? There's the beauty of the subjects, like the First Baptist Church in Amsterdam, NY, and then there's the actual cards themselves. You gotta hand it to Wilhelm II – those crafty pre-World War I Germans really new their stuff when it came it to lithography (heck, they invented the process). Nothing appeals to mankind like pretty pictures made of dots.

Which leads us to the Frederator cards contained herein. Scholars will want to debate for centuries the actual practical, historical, and aesthetic merits of these postcards. But listen: we used them to communicate ideas; we mailed them, in some cases, like, years ago; and they're cool-looking, too. Debate over.

So at the end of the day, these Frederator postcards ably meet my criteria of why I enjoy collecting postcards. To boot, they more than "up the cool quotient" for us collectors. So take pride, fellow deltiologists – Frederator postcards make it all okay.

Eric Homan
Burbank 2005

Finally, to my would-be enablers: when you come across any cards, series A, published by the Rotograph company, circa 1906, I'm your man. Thanks.

Eric Homan is the Vice President of Creative Affairs for Frederator Studios. In 1992, he joined Hanna-Barbera Cartoons in Hollywood and later became the creative director of its animation art department. When the cartoon company was folded into the Time-Warner family in late 1996, he was hired by Warner Bros. Studio Stores to continue overseeing the production of Hanna-Barbera artwork and collectibles. In 1998, Homan became the first employee of Frederator Studios.

Postcards from the Fred

An introduction by Jerry Beck

You are holding in your hands a rare piece of animation history.

Frederator Studios has been sending limited edition postcards to you, me and six hundred other animation bigshots for several years now. Some of you may have tossed them away – others may have sealed them in plastic to preserve as future collector's items. I myself have simply wrapped them in a rubber band and buried them safely, somewhere, in my animation image archive (a.k.a. my cluttered file cabinet). As an animation historian I've truly treasured these postcards because they represent a time capsule of an amazing period of animation creativity.

Fred Seibert's incubator program, *Oh Yeah! Cartoons* for Nickelodeon, is a rare opportunity for anyone with a funny idea, clever characters, and a fresh visual take to get a shot at creating the next potential Nicktoon superstar. Fred's number one priority is to let creators be creative – and let cartoonists be cartoonists.

Thus his *Oh Yeah! Cartoons* are more daring, original and creator driven than other network's pilot programs. And these postcards – which at first glance seem like a clever, but disposable, piece of advertising and promotion – are actually rare pieces of art, imagination and animation history.

And up until now, these postcards have been one of the industry's biggest secrets. Fred has 600 people on his mailing list and 200 people receive every third card – and nobody gets a complete set (unless you write an introduction for one of his books, like I'm doing).

That's why I'm especially delighted that Fred and Eric have decided to collect them all one place and publish them in this book once and for all. Now I can go to the shelf and look at these beauties anytime I want – without having to worry about wear and tear on my precious originals. Now they are organized by season and indexed by creator. It's much easier to enjoy them this way.

And what a treat. There are rare pieces by such notable talents as Seth McFarland, Tim Biskup, Dave Wasson, Vince Waller, Craig Kellman, Carlos Ramos, Miles Thompson and Alex Kirwan. Certain cards – notably the ones for *ChalkZone*, *My Neighbor is a Teenage Robot* and *The Fairly Oddparents* – are significant early takes on what would become successful long running Nickelodeon series. Other non-cartoon cards show off Fred's considerable sense of humor. The caricatures and collages representing the creative mindset at Frederator are inspiring and fun.

These postcards are also a throwback to the kind of animation ballyhoo practiced in the golden age of Hollywood cartoons – and rarely done today, especially for one-shots or pilots. Back in the classic days, cartoon shorts like *One Froggy Evening* (Warner Bros. Chuck Jones 1956), *King*

Size Canary (MGM, Tex Avery 1947) and *Rooty Toot Toot* (UPA, John Hubley 1952) would routinely have dedicated movie posters prepared for theatres – and studios required the cartoonists to create special art for publicity purposes. That really isn't done anymore. Frederator is perhaps the only studio still publicizing their cartoons in this unique manner. It's a tradition of film promotion that dates back to Gertie the Dinosaur – in fact, it dates back even further, to the days of the original nickelodeon theatres.

I guess that brings us full circle. The current generation of Nickelodeon animation artists have influenced modern day kids culture with their stylish designs, witty storyboards and savvy cartoon filmmaking. And this book represents a piece of this modern day animation history.

The thing I like most about this collection of postcard graphics is that it preserves the moment, celebrates the talent and reminds us of Frederator's pivotal role as a champion of funny cartoons.

Jerry Beck is the author of ten books on animation history including The Animated Movie Guide, The 50 Greatest Cartoons, *and* Looney Tunes: The Ultimate Guide. *He urges you to visit his website* www.cartoonresearch.com *and his blog* www.cartoonbrew.com *on a regular basis.*

The Fred Seibert Interview

By Joe Strike

If one man can be credited with *resuscitating American commercial animation from its near-death experience in the '80s and '90s, it would have to be Fred Seibert.*

After putting the then-new MTV on the map with a series of unforgettable, no-two-alike animated ID spots, he took over the creatively exhausted Hanna-Barbera studio and engineered a turnaround that brought some of the country's most innovative young animators to its doors. Their creations helped make another newborn cable network more than a place where old cartoons went to die. Moving onto an association with Nickelodeon, Fred proved his success was no fluke by midwifing a second batch of groundbreaking, creator-driven cartoons that helped cement Nick's dominance of the children's television market. Fred will often praise an associate or collaborator as being "an awesome judge of talent"- a description he more than deserves himself. With an eye toward the main chance that others have overlooked, and an instinctive understanding of both the creative and commercial potential of animated cartoons, Fred has a knack for making himself the right man at the right time. In late March and early April 2003, I had the pleasure of sitting down with Fred Seibert in his Fifth Avenue office where he heads Frederator, the animation company he started in 1997. I discovered that he is not shy about taking - or sharing - credit for his successes, or accepting blame for his failures. I also learned why he prefers cartoons over animation.

Joe Strike: *I've read a lot about you already, but can you give me the 10-cent recap how it all began?*

Fred Seibert: Sure. I started in the media business in college radio at Columbia University. I went from there to becoming an independent record producer, making primarily jazz and blues records.

That got into me into commercial radio, at WHN here in New York, which was then a country music station. I did advertising and promotion - that was my introduction to that part of the world. I was introduced to [MTV founder] Bob Pittman by my mentor, Dale Pon, who had been working with Bob in radio. I basically developed a career as "the branding guy" in cable television, primarily at MTV networks. My then-partner, Alan Goodman, and I introduced the whole notion of branding to cable television through our company Fred/Alan. We helped clients like Nickelodeon develop unique personalities that people could connect with emotionally. Nowadays it's a given, but back then branding was a new idea in TV promotion.

Then I went and became the president of Hanna-Barbera when we closed Fred/Alan. That started me in animation.

JS: *What was Hanna-Barbera like at the time?*

FS: A disaster. At the time I got there, in 1992, they no longer blanketed Saturday morning, and they hadn't had a hit since The Smurfs in 1983.

JS: *And the quality of what they were producing.*

FS: It wasn't the quality per se of what had happened at Hanna-Barbera, it was the fact that they clearly had lost touch with communicating with human beings and making things that people fell in love with. They didn't make hits. They had no idea what people wanted anymore.

JS: *Who was hot at that point?*

FS: Nickelodeon was new kid on block at that point; they had *Rugrats*, *Doug*, and *Ren & Stimpy*.

JS: *All three of which had very distinctive looks to them.*

FS: Look aside, they were all popular. On Saturday morning FOX was really the winner at that moment. Actually, a Hanna-Barbera show, *Tom and Jerry Kids* was one of their hits. We had just come out of the Pee-wee Herman phase, and *Teenage Mutant Ninja Turtles* was big, so there was a lot of stuff out there.

JS: 2 Stupid Dogs *came along at this point. [Note... as did* SWAT Kats, *a show we did not get to explore.]*

FS: I told people around me, if the way this place is going to be a machine, a widget producer, they put the wrong guy in the job. But I'm interested in people you think are fantastic. I was very interested specifically in animators you think are fantastic with ideas, not writers - I had a very specific lack of interest in writers - and I'm obviously interested in properties you're really thrilled about that you don't necessarily feel fits the system, whatever the system is.

One of the first things in was a guy named Donovan Cook with a thing called *2 Stupid Dogs*. Depending on how you look at it - either very intelligently or unbelievably stupidly - I greenlit the series on half a storyboard and Donovan's presence in the room.

It was an unbelievably unsuccessful show.

JS: *I enjoyed it; it had a sly sense of humor and was a real change of pace from most of what was on at the time.*

FS: You're one of the few.

JS: *What about the back-up feature,* Super Secret Secret Squirrel? *I thought that was a brilliant revival.*

FS: I told Donovan we'll make 26 *2 Stupid Dogs* shorts, but I'd really like to stick to the old Hanna-Barbera formula of a half-hour with three shorts, and I'd like the middle to be something else. Why don't we see if there's a great classic character we can do something with, and he came in with the squirrel.

For my future, a very interesting thing happened. I had assigned one of the older veterans at the studio to help Donovan because I knew it was a snake pit, and I didn't know enough to re-invent the system at that point. Donovan needed a guide to the system. Beyond that, he was not at all capable of handling a series. An animated series is a complex machine. From the outside it doesn't look complex - then you add on the complications of the Hanna-Barbera machine - and the kid was doomed.

So I gave him an older guy, someone who was 45 and had been in the business since he was 20. He was actually someone else's recommendation, but I had the sense he could work with young folk without depressing them. We assigned this guy, Larry Huber, to be his supervisor, his handler.

It quickly became obvious Donovan was not going to let Larry in on *2 Stupid Dogs* too well, and Donovan was going to be too busy to do anything other than set up *Super Secret Secret Squirrel.* Once Donovan set the stage - he had his people redesign the characters and they made a couple of key creative decisions - after that Larry took it and ran it. Larry showed himself to be something other than what I thought he was at the time, which was a capable line producer. I found out that one, he was an awesome spotter of talent. Two, he was willing to give that talent room to be what they had not been before - he was able to see an artist or director and say maybe they'd be good at story. And third, I found out he was a magical film story guy, which is not what those line producer types were known as - he was an unbelievable story guy.

Donovan turned out to be fantastic at a couple of things. He was an awesome spotter of talent as well. He brought in a new level of young talent into the system. Because I allowed him something the studio had never allowed before - letting young people be in charge of their own destiny - the crew that he brought in turned out to be incredibly important to my future; at least a couple of dozen key people from the crew turned out to be the nucleus of the new world order for us.

JS: *So you're at Hanna-Barbera now, you've turned this awesome...*

FS: I hadn't done anything at that point. Not near. I hadn't even made a dent into the system at that point. It was just like oh, here's another new guy in charge of wasting our money. That was really all that had happened there.

A lot of business stuff was going on in the meantime. We had to carve through lot of very complicated things to get Hanna-Barbera on a footing that would allow us to do anything. Luckily I had a number-two man, Jed Simmons, who spent an enormous amount of selfless hours fixing it, so it worked out really nicely.

So, the next big thing was *What A Cartoon!*

I had been a consultant to Nickelodeon for many years before going to Hanna-Barbera. In 1989, the Nickelodeon programming and business team came to me and said we really need to get into the original production] cartoon business - how do we do it?

I had never really done anything in cartoons. I was really just a neophyte, an interested media person, but I knew about the way *Looney Tunes*, theatrical cartoons had been made. I said, it seems to me that what they did was make a seven-minute cartoon, run it before a movie and, if people liked it, they made another one [featuring the same character.] If they didn't like it they stopped making it.

I suggested a system that I thought made some kind of sense, but I had no idea how to execute it, because I knew nothing about cartoons. As usual when you're a consultant, they took pieces of my idea and threw out the rest. The piece that they took, that turned out to be valuable for a couple of years at Nickelodeon, was that they made pilots, which was radically different from the way that Hollywood made cartoons for kids. And that's when you got *Ren & Stimpy*.

JS: *That led to* What A Cartoon!?

FS: When I got to Hanna-Barbera, I knew [Nickelodeon] hadn't done the system the way I wanted to do it because I didn't think pilots were the thing.

To me, pilots are things that you'll never show anybody and they're messy, they're all over the place, they're not disciplined.

My model for everything I've done successfully in the media

business, no matter what medium I've been in, whether I was a record producer or in radio was Berry Gordy's Motown. I loved the idea that they were all in a house and the recording studio was here, and the writing studios were here and the promotion department was here, and quality control - Berry Gordy's office - was up here, and when they needed an extra singer they went to the receptionist and said, do you sing - I love that.

I always loved the idea of a factory system where the goal of the factory was unique creative work; where you could discipline the execution process so that it didn't get out of control. I always thought you could get more good, interesting work out of that kind of creative system. My love of going to Hanna-Barbera was I always had the sense they had that system in the old days - and they had lost sight of it.

So I arrive knowing I want to make these short cartoons like *Looney Tunes* used to do. I knew Hanna-Barbera was not a place that talented people felt they belonged. Hanna-Barbera was a place for three kinds of people - people getting their first job, people on their last job or filling in between jobs, and people who really had a tough time getting jobs elsewhere.

So here I am, I know that no first-level creative person would ever come to Hanna-Barbera, and I knew I needed system to attract them, and where I could try out as many people as possible - and figure out who had the goods and who didn't.

I'd met John Kricfalusi in the meantime, We became very good friends. He told me lots of stuff - and I listened very carefully, I was a great student.

[And we] had a sister company that was starting a cartoon network. We're a new network, and advertisers and cable operators respect original programming, they don't respect library. If we're going to get distributors and advertisers we've got to do new stuff.

I actually don't have many talents, but I'm a good analyst, and I never do anything unless I know why I'm doing it. If I fail, it's because I didn't know why I was doing it to begin with. I had just made two series - *2 Stupid Dogs* and *SWAT Kats* - for 10 million bucks, and they failed within a week.

I said 'I have an idea how we can get publicity for 48 weeks. Let's make a new show every other week - and I can do it for 10 million. Let's make it like *Looney Tunes*.'

I had had my tutorial from John, I had spent a long time talking to Bill and Joe, not about Hanna-Barbera, but about *Tom and Jerry* and how they produced cartoons. I talked to Friz Freleng and a bunch of other people and they taught me how they made those shorts.

So I said 'we'll make a short cartoon every week. It'll be a new character every week, and you'll run it at your most popular time: primetime Sunday evenings just before a cartoon movie. We'll do it just like the old days, and every other week for two years you'll be able to get some publicity out of it. All of a sudden people will think [you] must be doing a lot of stuff."

Lo and behold, Cartoon Network bought it. So I called John and asked him who should I know? John gave me my first list.

JS: *Who was on it?*

FS: David Feiss, Eddie Fitzgerald, a guy named Tom Minton and four or five other guys whose names are escaping me. The only ones I wound up making deals with were Dave and Eddie, and Dave went the distance with *Cow and Chicken*, which was fantastic.

[And there] were 400 employees at Hanna-Barbera; a lot of the key talent that have gone far with me were people who were already at [the studio] when I got there.

Larry Huber [became the] supervising producer on *What A Cartoon!* He had supervised Donovan Cook on *2 Stupid Dogs*; I said 'Okay, you did such a great job with Donovan - now you've got 48 of them to supervise.' He felt like, 'Is this a promotion?!'

I told the Hanna-Barbera staff 'I know the business you've been in has been one where you do management and network bidding. They tell you what to do and you do it. I know you got into this business because you feel like you're talented and you have something to say. I'm here to make what you want to make.'

At that point in the industry, the business was such that the cartoonists believed that if they did have an idea the studio or network would take it from them and they would get nothing.

JS: *Work for hire.*

FS: Right. I made a deal with them saying if we do your thing you will get something. They had all been complaining to me the first couple of years I'd been there about this stuff. I prepared for a stampede at the door. No one showed up.

JS: *Was everyone there caught in a rut?*

FS: I think there was a combination of cynicism, pessimism, disinterest and purely the fact that most people want to do what they're told and complain about it rather than take the bull by the horns and do something for themselves.

A couple of guys that I actually went after who had expressed interest before said what will you pay me to make a storyboard. Well, we're not going to pay, this is your thing and we'll be interested in seeing what you have. 'But I'm a professional - I get paid to make a storyboard.' I said, yeah when you're doing my work you do that, but when you're doing your work... They completely missed the mark. After beating the bushes for weeks, one of the kids shows up at the door. At the time he was probably about 25. Larry Huber calls them the fists. They were doing props or storyboards or character designs and they do what they're told – they're a fist.

One of the fists turns up at the door and said I have an idea, can I pitch you my board with one of my other partners here. He pitched it to me - and it wasn't that good. But because he showed up first, he got a short. It turned out to be the worst short. But before it was even done, he came back again with another one, and it was a lot less worse - in terms of the pitch. He was enthusiastic and he had really learned things from the first, and I said let's do it - and it turned out to be the second worst short. He ended up doing I think five *What A Cartoon!* shorts.

JS: *You must've had faith in this guy.*

FS: Well, every time out of the box he improved. Most people when they come back to you the second time they're exactly the same or they go down. But this guy learned something every time out. By the time he was done his last short was probably in the top 25 - but still not the top. In my first season doing *Oh Yeah! Cartoons* for Nickelodeon I had one last slot to fill. He had been working on Johnny Bravo at the time and his contract was up. He called and said I'm available, I have another project to show you. We looked at it and green lit it, and that was *The Fairly OddParents* from Butch Hartman.

So the first place I went into was Hanna-Barbera and then I really started scanning the world. We just started putting our tentacles out, we called Ralph Bakshi out of nowhere and said Ralph, do you want to get back to your roots and he did. He's a character, but he was a very great character for us, he's larger than life.

JS: *Why shouldn't people who make cartoon characters...*

FS: - be characters, exactly. At the time, if you think about, there were only a couple of well-known animation people and he was one of them. That was a great feather in our cap that looked to people like it was all beginners, to have a couple of well known veterans like Ralph in the mix.

JS: *Didn't Bill [Hanna] or Joe [Barbera] do one as well?*

FS: They each did one for just that reason. In fact, Bill's was wonderful.

JS: *They must've enjoyed just getting hands-on and making a short again.*

FS: Absolutely. Joe wanted to know why he couldn't do all 48.

What A Cartoon! gave us *Dexter's Laboratory, The Powerpuff Girls, Cow and Chicken, Johnny Bravo, Courage the Cowardly Dog* – which, by the way, gave Hanna-Barbera its first Oscar nomination in the studio's history. The *Cow and Chicken* spin-off *I.M. Weasel,* and we had a compilation of the shorts themselves, the *What A Cartoon! Show*. So we had seven series, any one of which earned enough money for the company to pay for the whole program.

JS: *Basically a research and development program.*

FS: Then on top of it [we] reinvigorated the who comes in the studio equation. Now talented people wanted to show up. Some 5,000 people pitched us cartoons from all over the world. We got into business with Ralph Bakshi, with Bruno Bozetto, we got into business with a broad range of people who never would've given Hanna-Barbera a passing chance. We worked with people who were 70 years old, who were 20 years old. We turned on its head the perception the people in the community had of us. And by the way, we made almost a billion dollars worth of value for the company.

JS: *When did you decide to leave Hanna-Barbera?*

FS: First of all, understand that the day I got in there I said to everyone I know nothing about animation, and the likelihood that I will ever work in animation again outside the studio is virtually nil. My career has been characterized as having no career. I was like a ping-pong ball in a wind tunnel. Wherever I went where I thought I could do something interesting I did it.

I went to work for an entrepreneur - Ted Turner - who I knew was going to indulge my entrepreneurial impulses. I knew when [Turner] merged with Time Warner that was not going to happen anymore. I was not going to be in a company as small as Turner was.

JS: *A much more corporate culture.*

FS: It was just a completely different culture, and it was not one that indulged people like me. I knew that my time was up, so I left with the merger.

And [then] I made a deal as an independent producer of new animation for Nickelodeon.

JS: *That's when Frederator was born?*

FS: Yeah. I left Hanna-Barbera in October 1996 and Frederator started January 1997.

JS: *You credit people like Larry Huber as having a knack for recognizing and developing talent; it sounds like you share that ability with him.*

FS: It's something I'm interested in. As an independent producer it's required, because the only reason that companies make deals with producers is that producers know something they don't. And most of the time the thing that producers know and companies don't is how to root out talent and nurture and develop them into something valuable for the company.

JS: *How do you find talent? Or do you wait for it to come to you?*

FS: No, you can never wait. Well you can wait; big companies wait. The studios wait, the networks wait, they literally sit there in their offices and take phone calls from agents. As an independent you can't afford that, because frankly you're the last one on their phone list - you're never first.

I'm analytical. I'm not very disciplined, but I'm very organized - I'm a systems guy. When I have to deal with an issue like rooting out talent, I develop a system. Within that system I figure out how to put out a call to the greater community, saying I'm looking, and now I've developed a system for them to come in and to judge, which is ultimately what you have to do.

JS: *You have a brain trust you'll call and say 'I have a project here that I need you to come in and give me some feedback on.' People like Kricfalusi?*

FS: Yeah, absolutely. Literally when I started *What A Cartoon!*, in part based on things I learned from John Kricfalusi, he was the first one I called. I said, John you'll never believe it, I'm doing exactly what you believe should be done.

If anyone should get credit for changing the name of the game in traditional cartooning, it should be John Kricfalusi. There were also the Mike Judges of the world and a few other people. But for people who work in the commercial grind, making commercial cartoons - John Kricfalusi's the man. He changed the game. He wanted to make the kinds of cartoons Hollywood wanted to make, in the system they wanted to make it, but he wanted them to be passionate and successful.

When I started Frederator and *Oh Yeah! Cartoons*, my first talent pool were the people that I had already done stuff with that I thought were special, but maybe hadn't hit the mark yet. There were people that didn't show up in time for the *What A Cartoon!* One of the most interesting ones was Larry Huber who had been my supervising producer for *What A Cartoon!* I asked him to leave Hanna-Barbera and come over with me like a shot in the dark and be my partner in the cartoons. Here I am, I haven't been in the business five years, I'm really young, younger than he is. He said, Well I'll be your supervising producer. I said, No, be my co-executive producer.

What Larry did was put a team together. Larry put together a real creative team, which is very smart.

The first pool of talent for *Oh Yeah!* came from *What A Cartoon!* and Hanna-Barbera. Then [we] put the word out in the community and people started coming in. But then the next place, which is the most obvious, was our own crew.

When we give something to a creator we say, 'Here are the people that are in our shop right now' - and we started with five people – 'here are the five we have, do you want to work with any of them or who do you want to bring in? So, one by one, as we signed creators, they started bringing in people.

Within that team we already had they saw the opportunity and now the crew started coming in and pitching shorts.

JS: *The opposite of your experience at Hanna-Barbera.*

FS: Well by that point, *Dexter's*, *Johnny Bravo* and *Cow & Chicken* were on the air. We now had three hit examples of what could happen. So it was no longer an experiment. It was now like, 'Ohmigod, if I can get into this thing, I could go to the top.'

JS: *Where and when did* Oh Yeah! Cartoons *run?*

FS: Nickelodeon scheduled *Oh Yeah!* on Friday nights in an hour block with another anthology show, *Kablaam!* (basically the indie version of Oh Yeah!). Bob Mittenthal, *Kablaam!*'s producer worked with a lot of independent animators, people outside of the Hollywood mainstream, and had a much more writer-driven approach than I did.

The two shows complemented one another: *Kablaam!* gave Nickelodeon the cream of the indie crowd, and we gave them the cream of the commercial filmmaking world, the people who have come to Hollywood to make cartoons, not animation. I'm a cartoon maker, I'm interested in cartoons and I have a distinctive view of them as different from animated films.

JS: *What successes came out of* Oh Yeah!*?*

FS: We made 51 shorts, 51 original *Oh Yeah!*s, plus another 49 or 50 sequels of the best ones. Someone would come in, Larry Huber would come in with *ChalkZone*, and once we saw the film, we said why don't we make six more. Or a guy named Dave Wasson - who went on to do *Time Squad* for Cartoon Network - would come in and make *The Goose Lady*, which was basically like a *Fractured Fairy Tale*, and we said, 'Why don't you make three more.'

So far - and I don't think we're anywhere near the end of this process - *Fairly OddParents* and *ChalkZone* began as *Oh Yeah!* shorts. The *ChalkZone* series launched with the highest debut ratings in Nickelodeon history. Rob Renzetti's *My Life as a Teenage Robot* was an *Oh Yeah!* short. We made seven or eight *Super Santa* shorts. That project has skipped animation for the time being, and is being developed as a live-action feature with its creator Mike Bell.

I think there's more to come. We're talking Nickelodeon into taking a second look at a few others, because if that's four out of 51, you still have 47 to look at closely. We started in January of 97 and here we are in March of 2003 and we've only gotten four into series. We created more original characters for air in three years than almost everyone else combined in a five-year period. It takes a while to absorb that. We're not producing any new character shorts at the moment, which I'm fine with.

JS: *What else was Frederator doing at time?*

FS: We made two animated features for Nickelodeon when they thought they were going to launch a series of original television movies called *NickFlicks*. One was *The Electric Piper*, which was a contemporary story with the pied piper as Jimi Hendrix, [conceived and] written by Bill Burnett.

The second one was directed by John Eng, who is now directing the third *Rugrats* movie. We took the title 'Around the World in 80 Days' and wrote a new story to it. It wound up being called *Globe Hunters*, and by the way I think it was the most beautiful animated made for TV movie I've ever seen. It's stunning. Aside from being a good director, John Eng is one of the most amazing stylists you've ever seen.

In 1999 and 2000 we greenlit *The Fairly OddParents* and *ChalkZone* series. Right around that time I decided to leave L.A. My wife and I had two small children that we wanted to raise in New York. Nickelodeon was gracious enough to allow me to remote control my role in these series.

Luckily, [we have] very high-level executors, or in this case creator-executors like Butch, Larry or Bill. At the point we go to series they don't really need me - or at least we hope they don't really need me. So it worked out very well that they produced their series and only occasionally do I have to be involved.

I didn't get into animation until I was 41 years old. I always looked at it like a temporary thing that I was doing because someone asked me to do it. It seemed like fun at the time, and I thought I could learn something.

Two years ago, right around the beginning of 2001, I looked up and I took stock. I had a couple of small kids, I had to figure out what I was going to do for the next 20 years. I had actually gotten further with this animation thing that I'd gotten with almost anything else. I've enjoyed it more than anything else, I love the talent, I'm a big fan of the talent. And at this point in my life I seem to have become financially productive for the networks that I work with.

JS: *Which opens all the doors.*

FS: Probably for the first time in my life I decided to be very focused and give production the majority of my activity. I started making calls again and said, I'm back in the game in a big way, let's figure out what to do.

I'm more actively pursuing and developing animation projects than ever before. In the meantime, we've launched our fourth Nickelodeon series. We produce or have more series on their air than anyone.

Nickelodeon is not just number one, it's number one by a factor of three or four. They've got about half the kids TV market, broadcast and cable, which is pretty awesome. But I had a fantastic time with Cartoon Network and all those people, they're great people. I like them a lot, there's no problems - they're just my competition now.

JS: *But still good relationships.*

FS: Absolutely, and by the way, our first hits continue to thrive on that network so I feel very good about that.

JS: *They're your kids but they're grown up and on their own.*

FS: Exactly. Now we're pursuing a number of different things. We have a bunch of movie projects that we're developing. In certain ways I'm very forward thinking, but in other ways I'm very conservative, and I always felt that the Disney method of making [animated] movies, which was wonderful, was but one method of making movies.

JS: *How would you describe that method?*

FS: Florid. Orchestral. Large. Classic. But, you know, that's like saying the only way to make a hit record is the way that Nelson Riddle and Frank Sinatra did. It's wonderful, but it's never the only way.

JS: *It's the stories, the characters.*

FS: And as a partner of mine here says, there are no little budgets, there are just little movies. I really believe that the low budget animated movie is an underestimated opportunity. The Rugrats-type movies cost more than $20 million to produce, but I think there's still an opportunity at lower budget levels to have big hit movies.

JS: *You didn't work on the Rugrats films.*

FS: That's Klasky-Csupo, and God bless them, they've done a fantastic job. I wouldn't know how to do what they do.

I'm a cartoon guy not an animation guy. They're animation people, you know. Right now I'm in development on five family-oriented features at this low budget level. They'll use television techniques, overseas studios, but stunning talent to do it.

JS: *You've made a distinction several times now between cartoons and animation. I sort of get the idea, but how would you define it?*

FS: Animation is a production technique. It does not define creatively or emotionally anything. It defines a very wide range of things. Minority Report had animation in it, the Vin Diesel movies have animation in them, Star Wars has animation. What the hell is it - it's a technique. It's like saying film.

Cartoons define for me a couple of key things... they're funny, they tend to be short, they tend to be character-driven, not story-driven; there's a design factor to it. And to me, the most subtle, but maybe one of the most important is they use music as a character, rather than as a support mechanism.

I think you'll agree when you hear a great cartoon score -

and, by the way, I don't just define a score as being by Carl Stallings, it can be Hoyt Curtin at Hanna-Barbera - you can actually read characters and action by just hearing the score. So score has a radically different role in cartoons than it does in almost any other kind of filmmaking.

I also define it as lots of physical humor. In my very narrow definition, the words fill in the gaps between the pictures rather than vice-versa; seven minutes long - that's cartooning.

When I'm talking with my development group about these animation features I want to do, the family ones, and they walk in with the Sleeping Beautys of the world or some such - I say, I don't do that. My natural space in life is cartooning. The talent that I've developed over a 10-year period consists of cartoonists, not animators. I want creative projects that take advantage of where my natural understanding is and where my talent goes.

Joe Strike is a New York City-based writer/producer with a lifelong interest in animation.

This interview was originally published online in Animation World Magazine *on July 15, 2003, and August 15, 2003. Republished with kind permission under limited license* *Special thanks to Sarah Baisley, Ron Diamond, Joe Strike, Heather Kenyon, and Dan Sarto.*

NICKELODEON PRESENTS THE FIRST SEASON OF

OH YEAH! CARTOONS!

Created by FRED SEIBERT

Apex Cartoon Props & Novelties ★ Ask Edward ★ Max
Blotto ★ Cat & Milkman ★ ChalkZone ★ Cop & Donut
Enchanted Adventures ★ Harvey Kurtzman's Hey Look!
Hobart ★ Hubbykins vs. Sweetiepie ★ Jelly's Day
Jamal the Funny Frog ★ Kitty the Hapless Cat
Microcops ★ Mother Goose: the Real Stories
Thatta-Boy ★ The F-Tales ★ The Feelers ★ ZooMates
Teddy & Art ★ That's My Pop ★ Protecto 5000
Olly & Frank ★ Pete Patrick Private Investigator
Twins Crimson & Those Amazing Robots
Tutu the Superina ★ Super Santa ★ What is Funny?
The Fairly Oddparents ★ The Man with No Nose
Youngstar 3

★ A FREDERATOR PRODUCTION ★

Executive Producers: LARRY HUBER & FRED SEIBERT

OH YEAH! original cartoons since 1998

Series 1 Postcards 1998-1999

< Designed and printed by Hatch Show Print

Illustration by Dynamic Duo
Color by Patrick Raske

Painting by Tim Biskup
Logo Design by Carlos Ramos

Created by Bill Burnett & Larry Huber
Illustration by Carlos Ramos

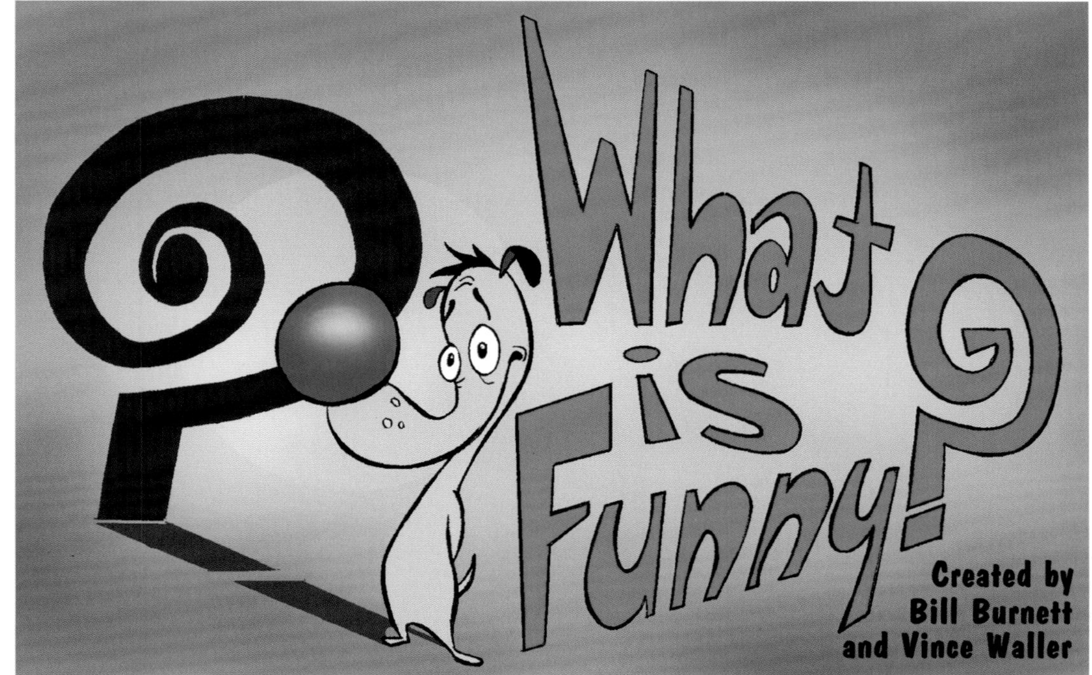
What is Funny?
Created by
Bill Burnett
and Vince Waller

Created by Miles Thompson

Created by Rob Renzetti

Created by Alex Kirwan

Created by Greg Emison & Bill Burnett

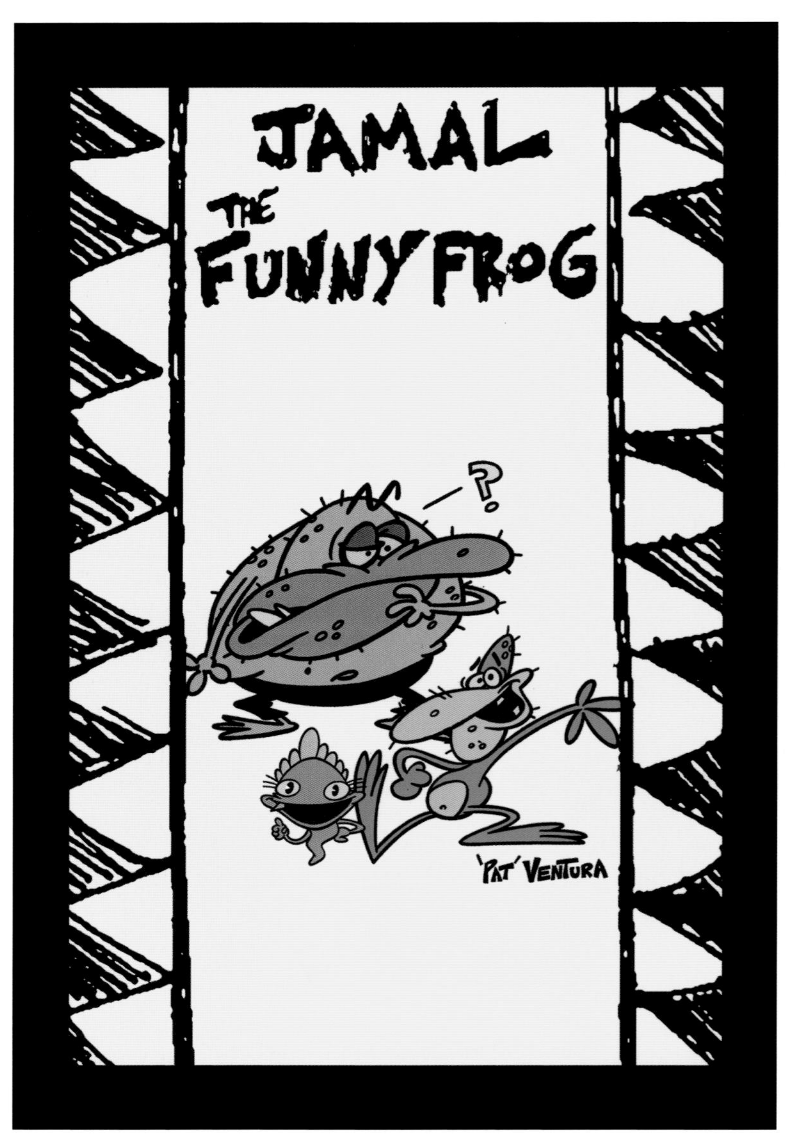

Created by 'Pat' Ventura

Created by Alex Kirwan

Created by John Eng

HOBART ©
Created by Bill Burnett and Greg Emison

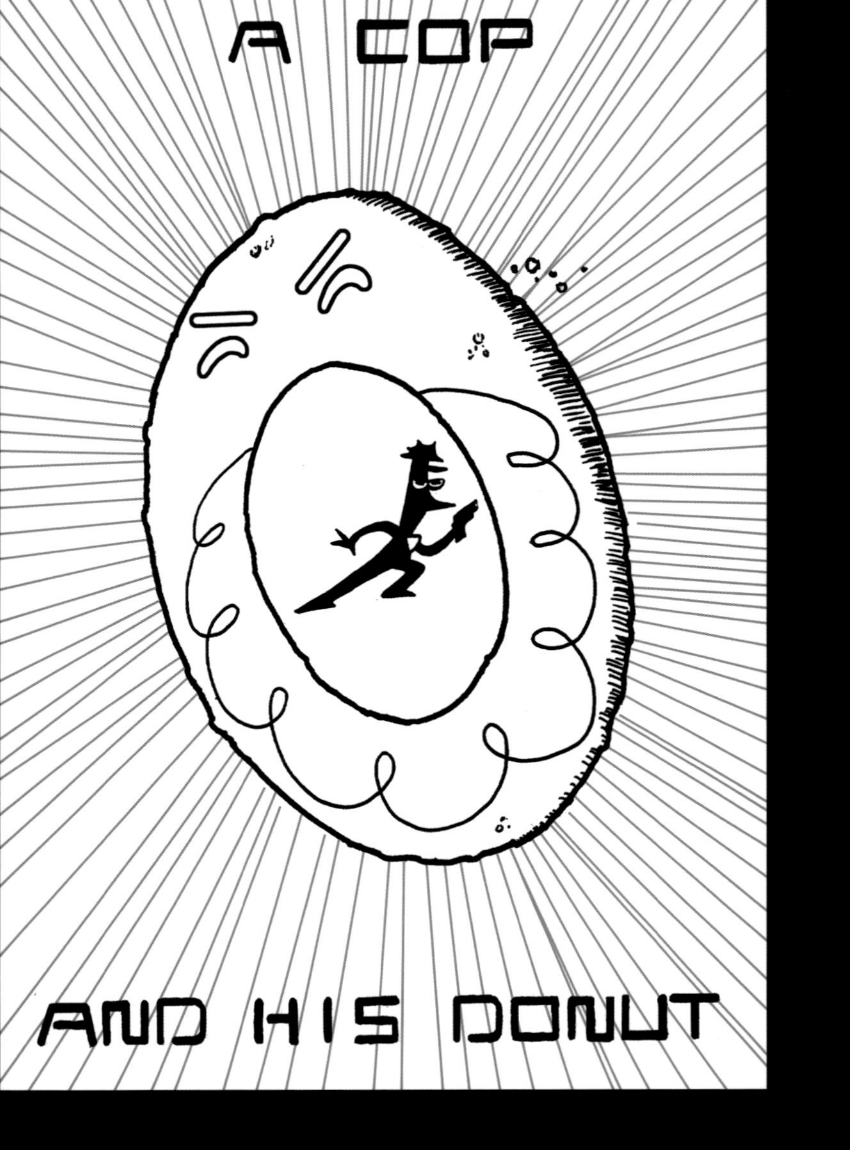
A COP
AND HIS DONUT

Created by Byron Vaughns

Created by Dave Wasson

Created by Bill Burnett

Created by Vincent Waller

Created by Dave Wasson

Created by Carlos Ramos

OLLY
&
FRANK
A CARTOON BY BOB BOYLE

THE
FAIRLY
ODDPARENTS!
CREATED BY: BUTCH HARTMAN!

Created by Rob Renzetti

Created by Larry Huber

Created by Zac Moncrief

Created by Mike Bell

Created by Larry Huber

Created by Rob Renzetti

THAT'S MY POP!
"THERE'S A DINOSAUR IN THE HOUSE"
ALL TALKING
*ALL COLOR
COMEDY
CARTOON
'PAT' VENTURA

ENCHANTED
ADVENTURES

Created by Miles Thompson

Created by Harvey Kurtzman
Adapted by Vincent Waller

Created by Dave Wasson

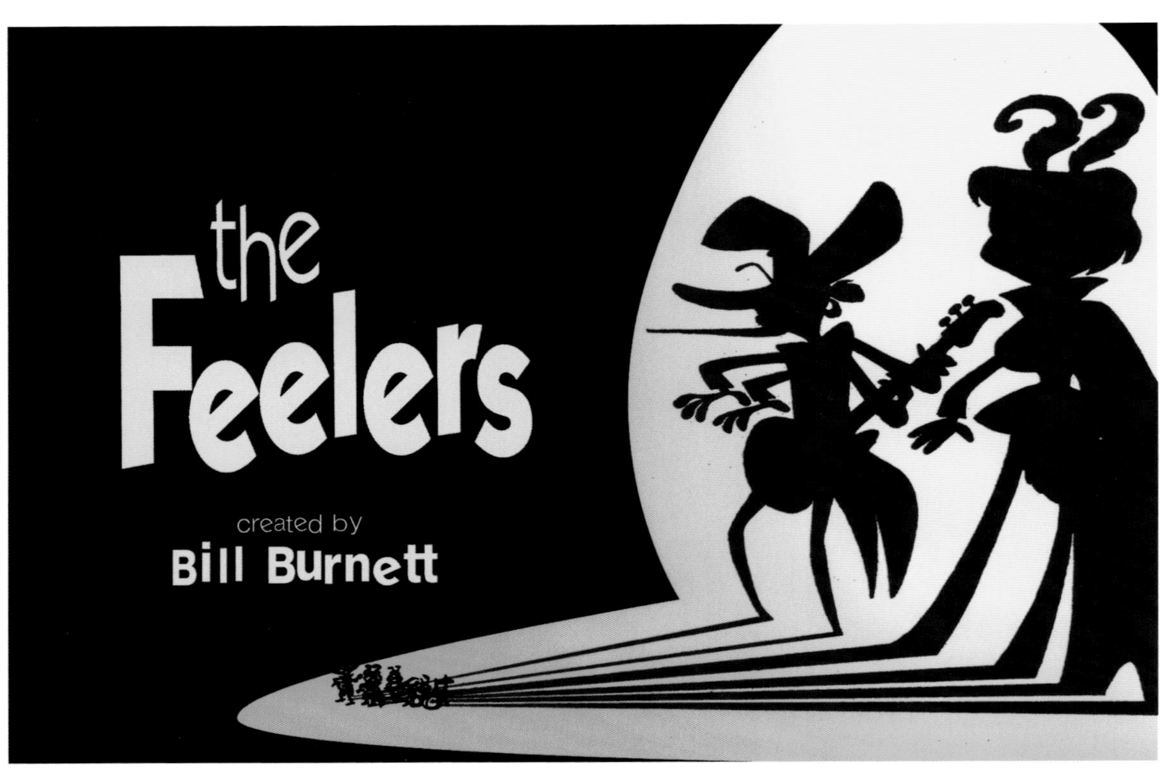

Created by Bill Burnett

Created by Dave Wasson

SETH MACFARLANE'S
LIFE IN THE BIG CITY
ZOOMATES!

Created by John Eng

Illustration by Mike Rogers

NICKELODEON
PRESENTS
THE SECOND SEASON OF

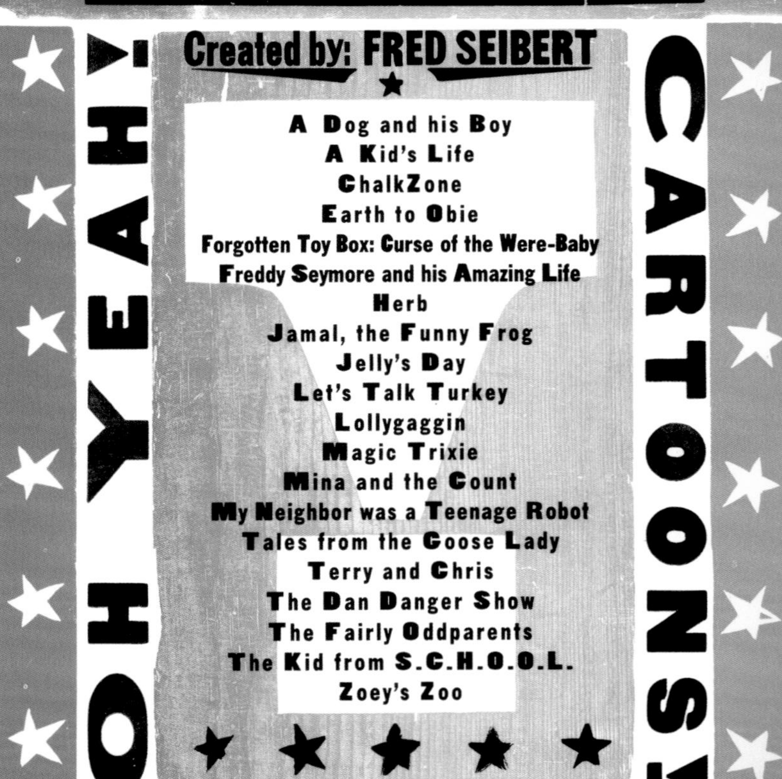

OH YEAH!
Created by: FRED SEIBERT
A Dog and his Boy
A Kid's Life
ChalkZone
Earth to Obie
Forgotten Toy Box: Curse of the Were-Baby
Freddy Seymore and his Amazing Life
Herb
Jamal, the Funny Frog
Jelly's Day
Let's Talk Turkey
Lollygaggin
Magic Trixie
Mina and the Count
My Neighbor was a Teenage Robot
Tales from the Goose Lady
Terry and Chris
The Dan Danger Show
The Fairly Oddparents
The Kid from S.C.H.O.O.L.
Zoey's Zoo
CARTOONS!

A FREDERATOR INCORPORATED PRODUCTION
Executive Producers: LARRY HUBER & FRED SEIBERT
OH YEAH!
Original Cartoons
since
1998
Hatch Show Print
• m. fred

Series 2 Postcards 1999-2000

< Designed and printed by Hatch Show Print

Illustration by Carlos Ramos

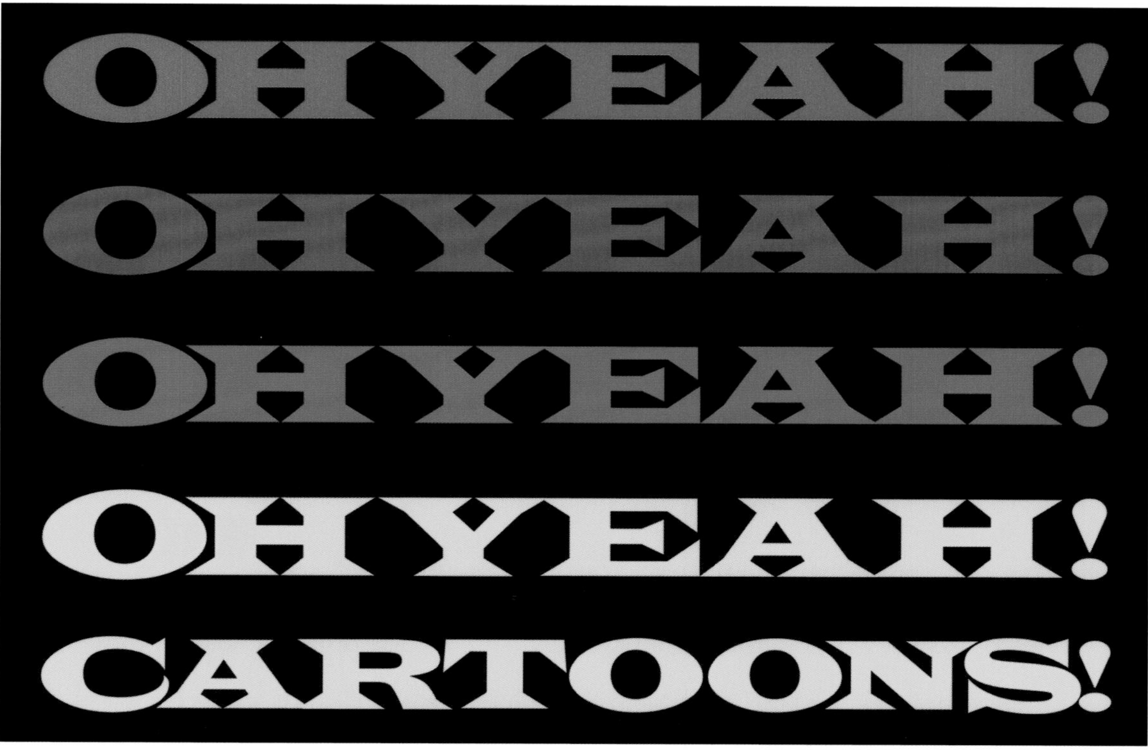
OHYEAH!
OHYEAH!
OHYEAH!
OHYEAH!
CARTOONS!

Created by Larry Huber & Bill Burnett

Created by Ken Kessel

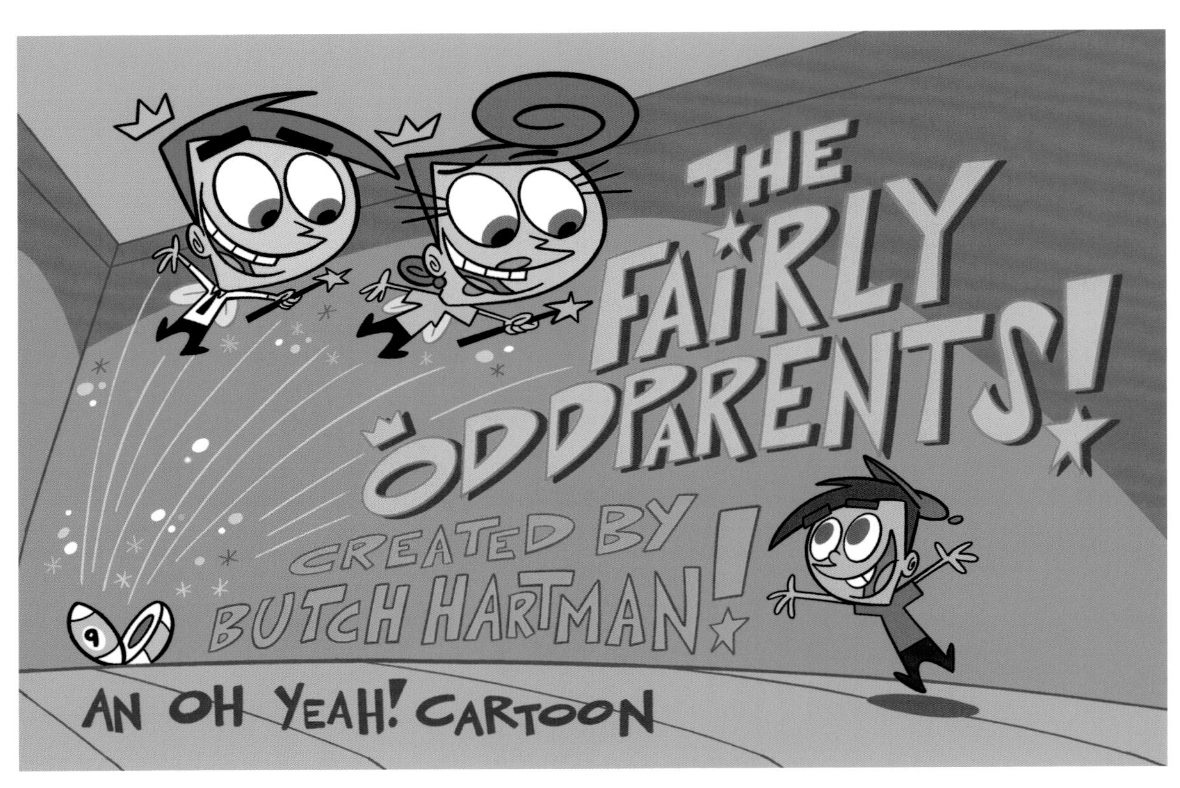

Created by Butch Hartman

Created by Alex Kirwan

Created by Dave Wasson

Created by Tim Biskup

JAMAL
THE FUNNY FROG
CREATED AND DIRECTED BY
'PAT' VENTURA
ALL-TALKING COMEDY CARTOONS IN COLOUR

Created by 'Pat' Ventura

Created by Bill Riling & Bob Boyle

RESURRECTED BY ROB RENZETTI

Created by Guy Vasilovich

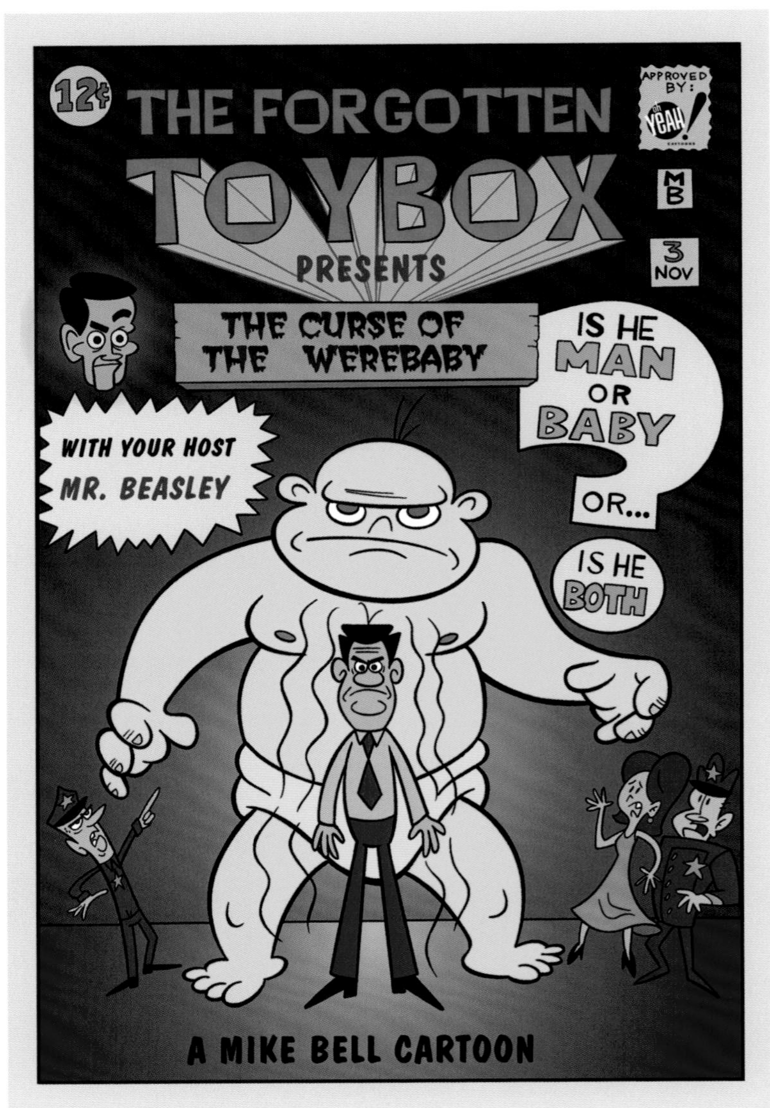

Created by Mike Bell

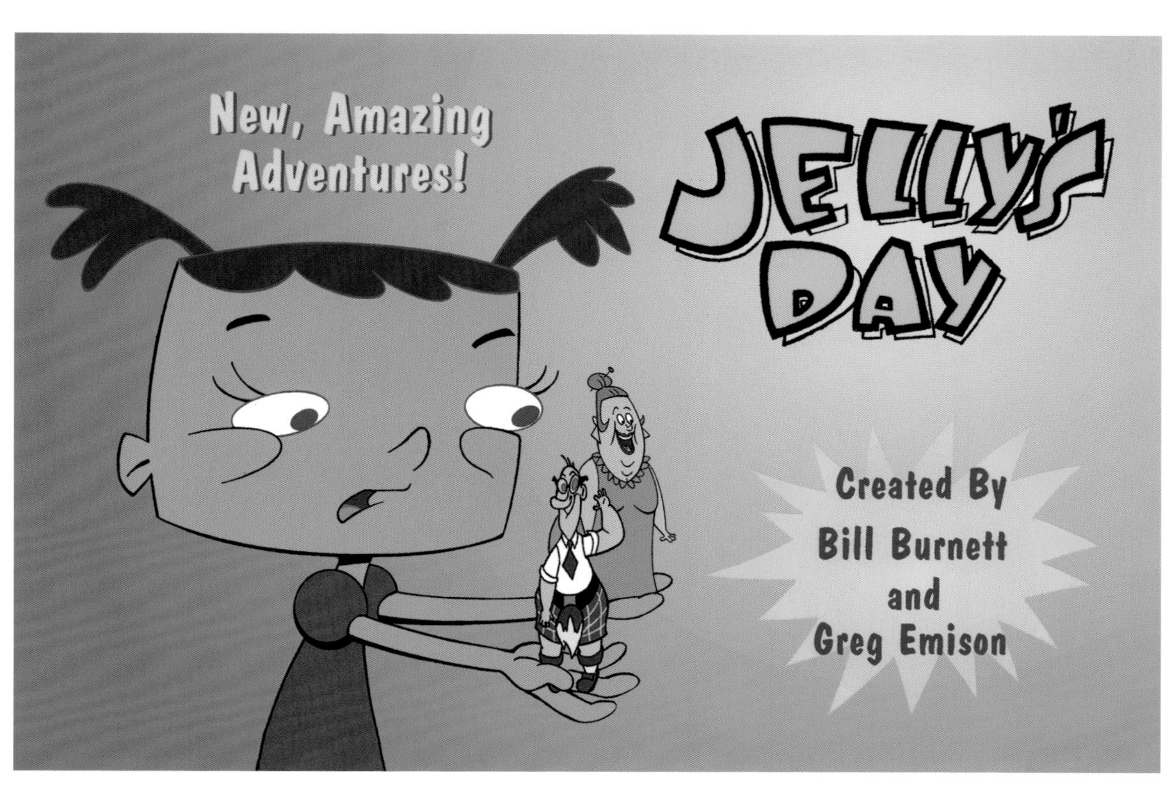

Created by Bill Burnett & Greg Emison

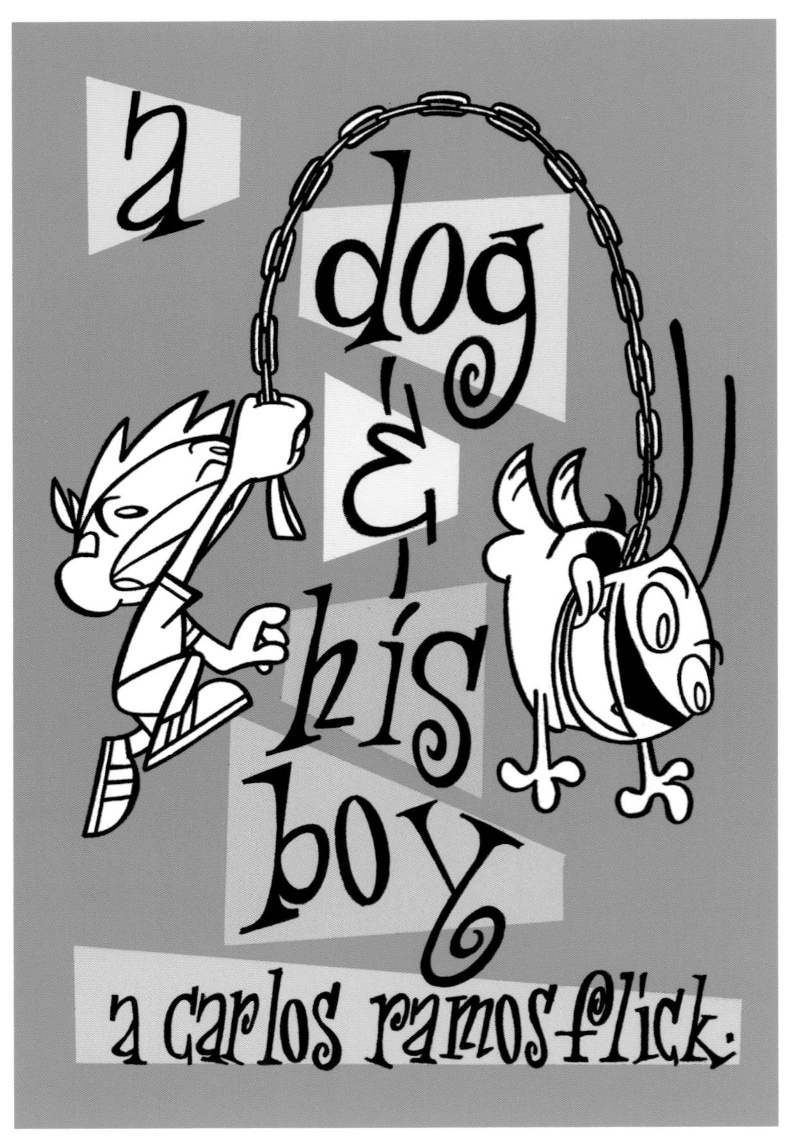

Created by Carlos Ramos

Created by Guy Vasilovich

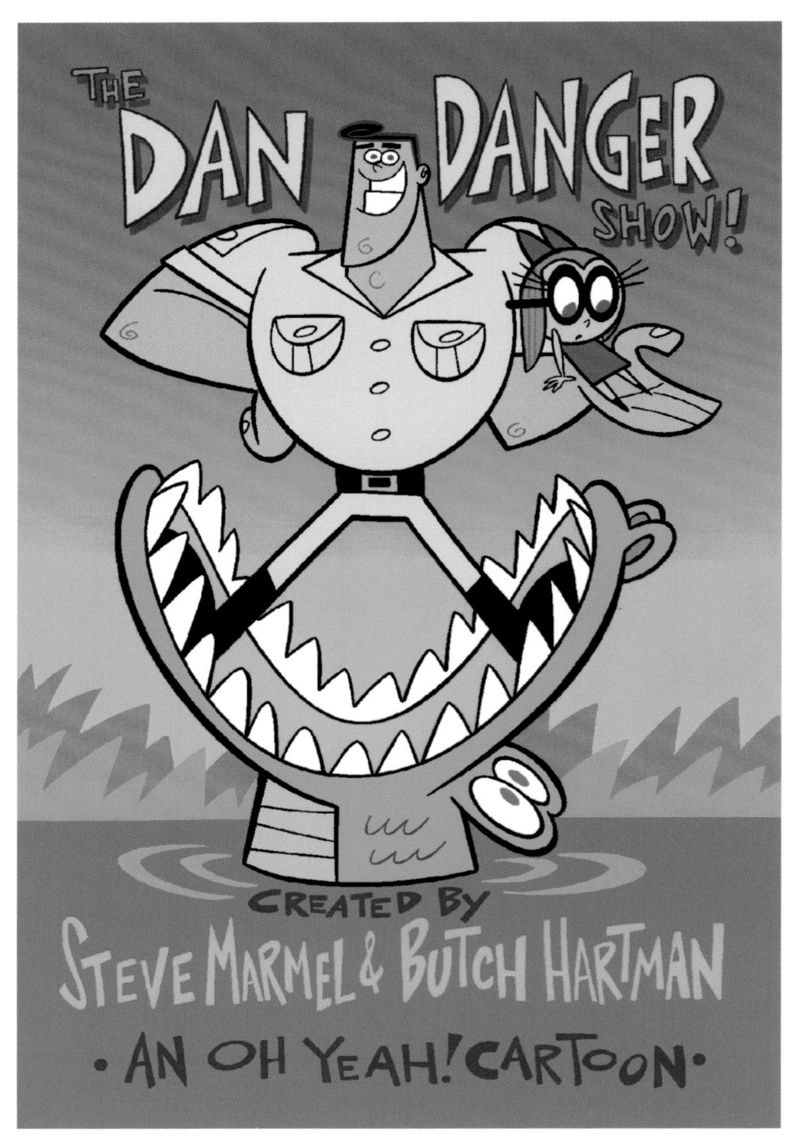

Created by Steve Marmel & Butch Hartman

Created by John Reynolds
Illustration by Butch Hartman

Created by Vincent Waller

Created by Amy Anderson & David Burd

Created by Rob Renzetti

HERB
HE WILL NOT BE PUSHED
FILED
STAMPED
INDEXED
BRIEFED
DEBRIEFED
OR NUMBERED!
HIS LIFE IS HIS OWN!
CREATED BY ANTOINE GUILBAUD

Created by Antone Guilbaud

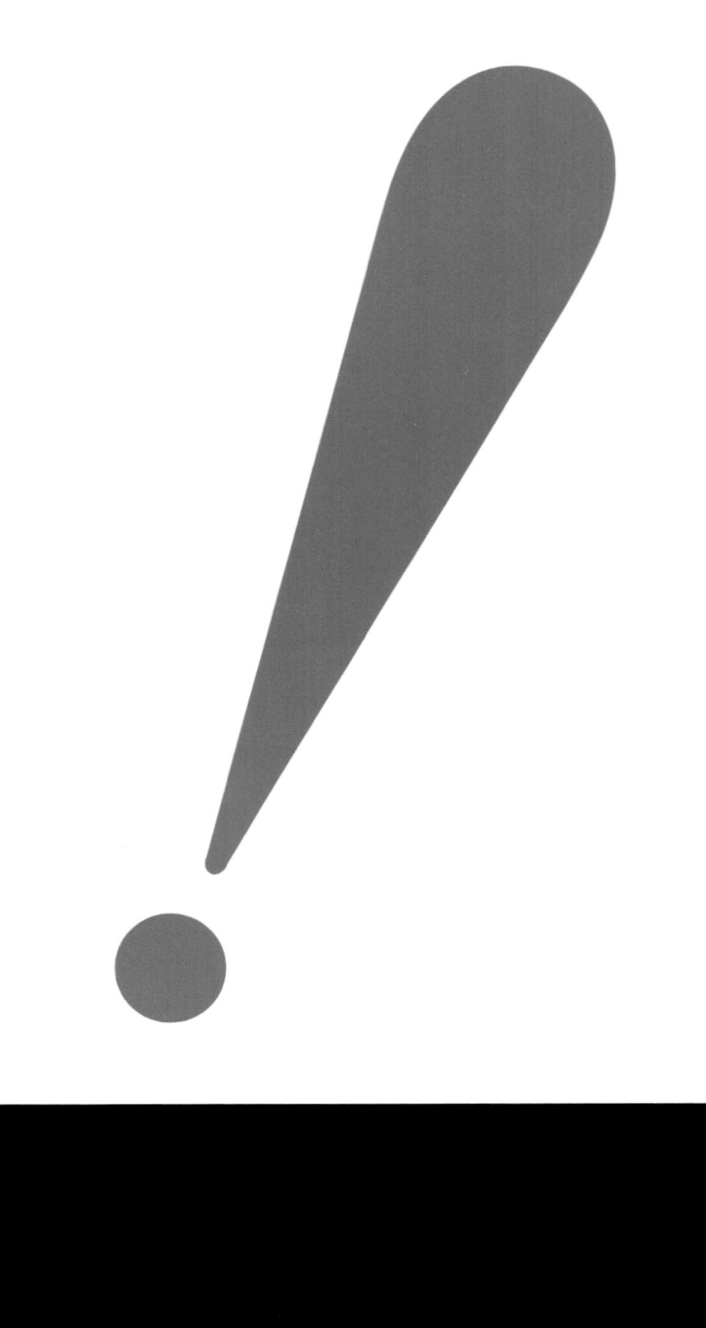

NICKELODEON PRESENTS THE THIRD SEASON OF

OH YEAH! CARTOONS

Created by Fred Seibert

A Kid's Life
Baxter and Bananas
The Dan Danger Show
Elise
The Fairly Oddparents
Jamal, the Funny Frog
The Kameleon Kid
Moville Mysteries
The Semprini Triplets
Sick and Tired
Skippy Spankerton
Super Santa
Tales from the Goose Lady
The Tantrum

A FREDERATOR PRODUCTION
EXECUTIVE PRODUCERS: LARRY HUBER & FRED SEIBERT

OH YEAH! ORIGINAL CARTOONS SINCE 1998

HATCH SHOW PRINT ★ NASHVILLE, TN. - cdg

Series 3 Postcards 2002

< Designed and printed by Hatch Show Print

Y
oh yeah! cartoons
3rd Season

oh YEAH!
CARTOONS

ORIGINAL CARTOONS SINCE 1998 EXECUTIVE PRODUCERS FRED SEIBERT AND LARRY HUBER

Created by Mike Bell

Created by John Fountain

Created by Steve Marmel & Butch Hartman

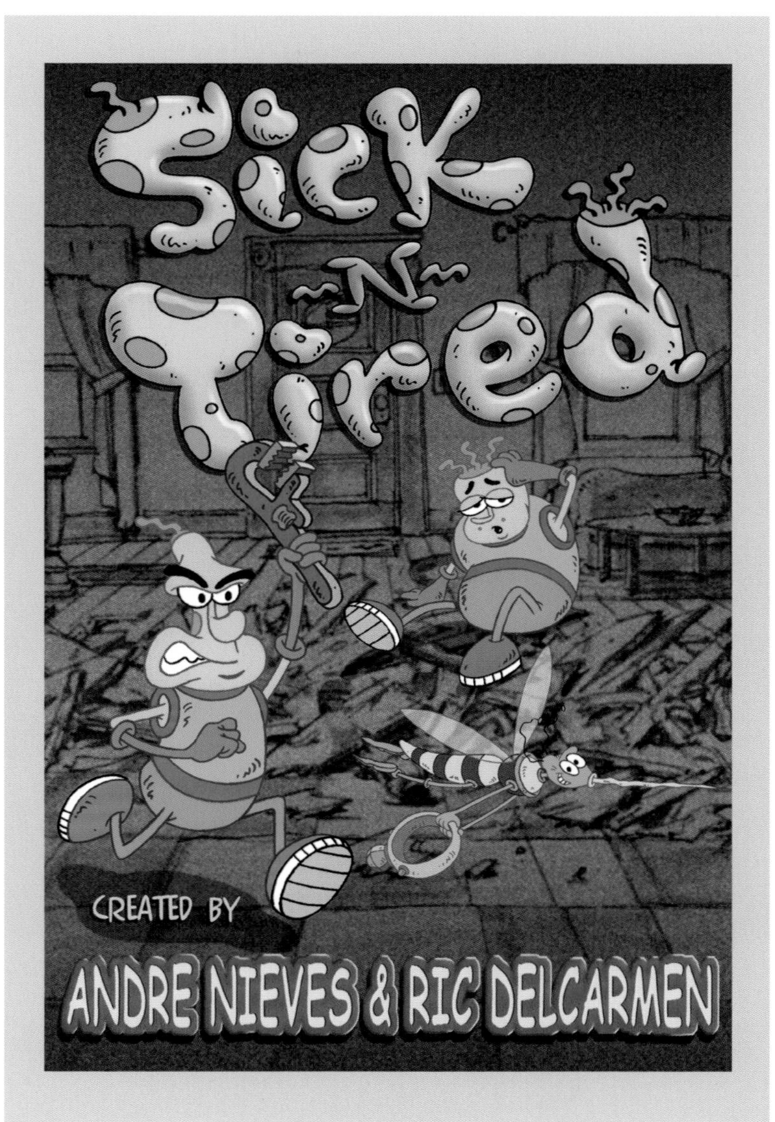

Created by Andre Nieves & Ric Delcarmen

Created by Dave Wasson

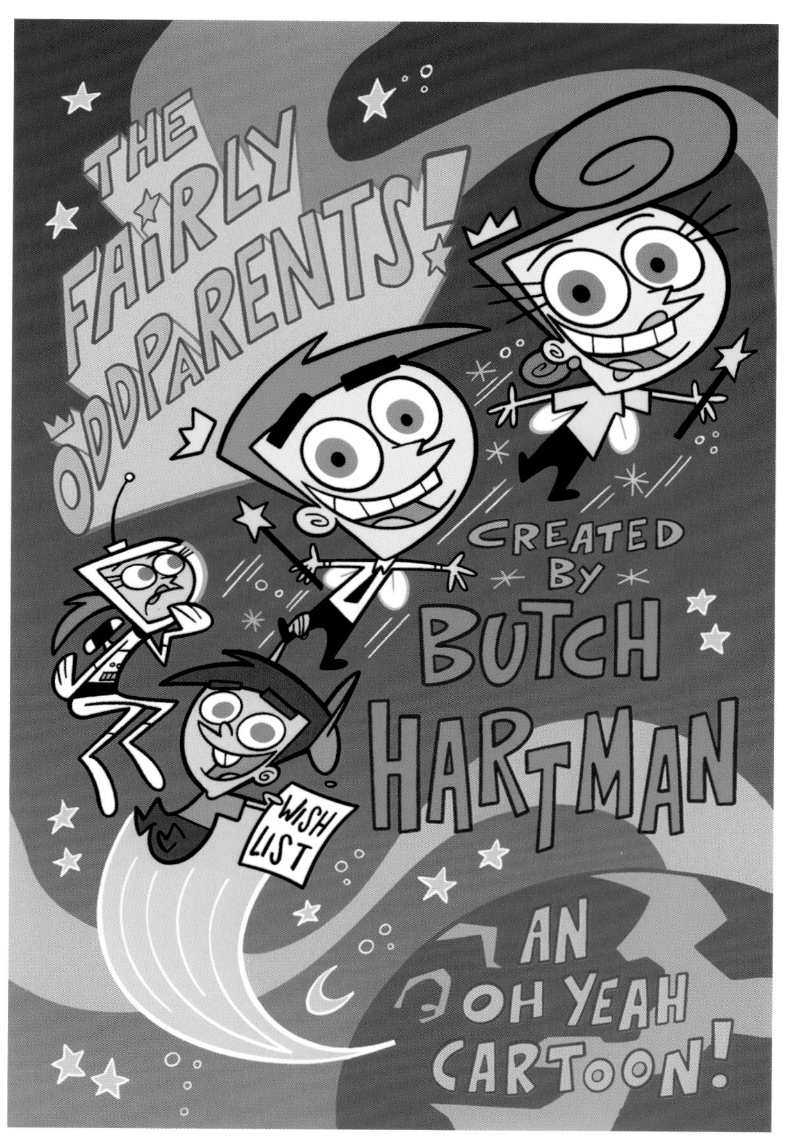

Created by Butch Hartman

Created by Eric & Michelle Bryan

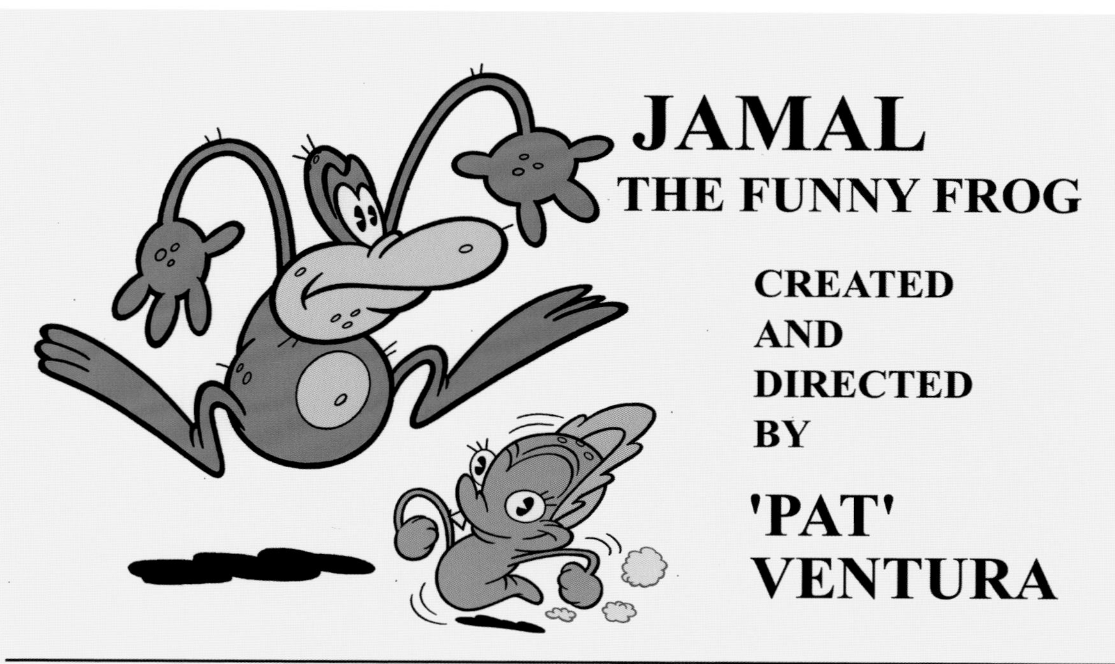

JAMAL
THE FUNNY FROG
CREATED
AND
DIRECTED
BY
'PAT'
VENTURA
ALL-TALKING COMEDY CARTOONS IN COLOR

Created by 'Pat' Ventura

Created by Guy Vasilovich

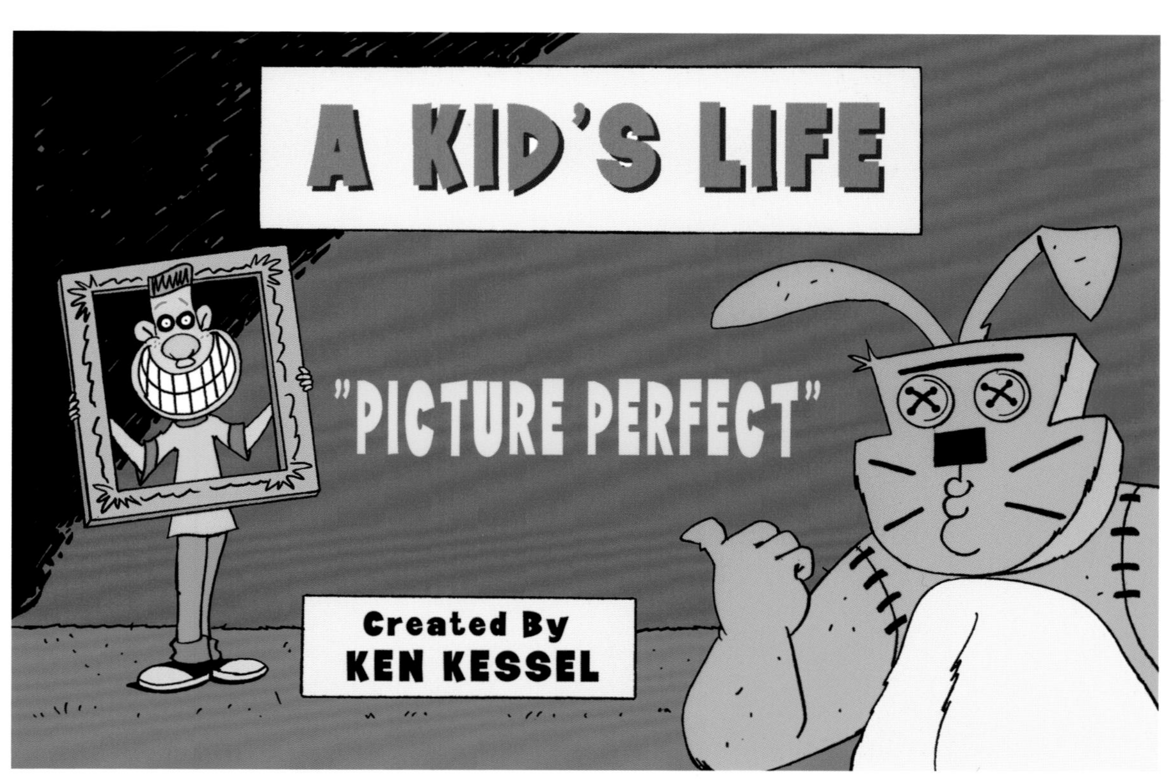

Created by Ken Kessel

Created by Zac Moncrief

Created by Jaime Diaz & Russell Mooney

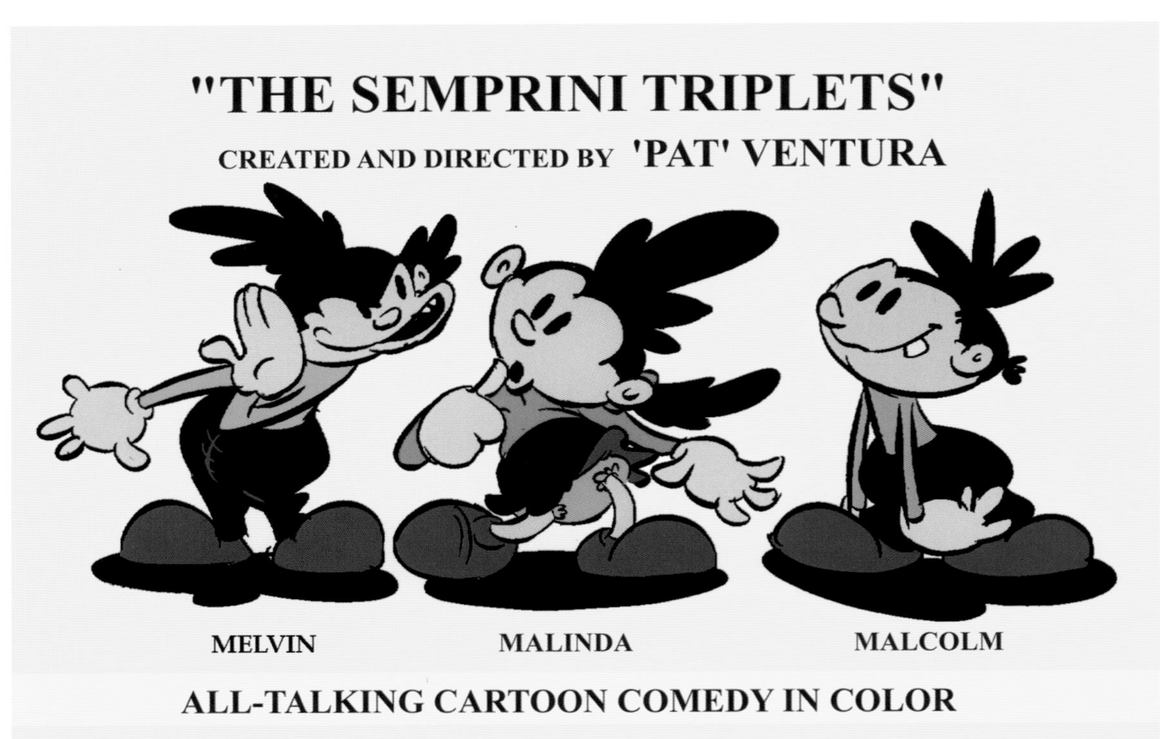

Created by 'Pat' Ventura

Created by Guy Vasilovich

?: What is FREDERATOR INCORPORATED ?

A: Fred Seibert set up FREDERATOR INCORPORATED as a CARTOON production company specializing in FUNNY, fantastic, innovative, provo-

?: What is FREDERATOR INCORPORATED ?

A: Fred Seibert has assembled the largest working team of ON-THE-AIR filmmakers creating their own CARTOONS. The *talent* includes animators right out of school (OR IN SCHOOL, IN THE CASE OF ONE 11 YEAR OLD CREATOR)

?: What is **FREDERATOR INCORPORATED** ?

A: *Talent.* You might have noticed that traditional Hollywood sys-tems of production don't always SUR-FACE the best stuff. Or most **SUCCESS-FUL.** *Well, we noticed,* **so we dec-**

?: How many **CARTOONS** are there at **FREDERATOR INCORPORATED** ?

A: Since 1998 we've produced **THREE** animated series (*Oh Yeah! Cartoons!*, ChalkZone, and **The Fairly Oddparents**), **54** original characters, **99** short films, **TWO** movies (The Electric Piper and Globehunters: An Around the World in 80 Days Adventure) and

Series 4 Postcards
2003

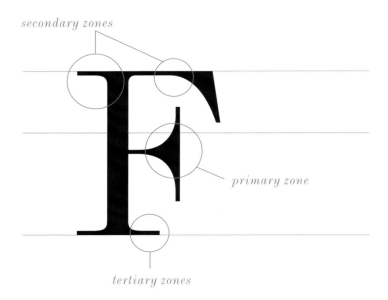

secondary zones

primary zone

tertiary zones

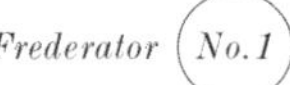

EROGENOUS ZONES OF A LETTER

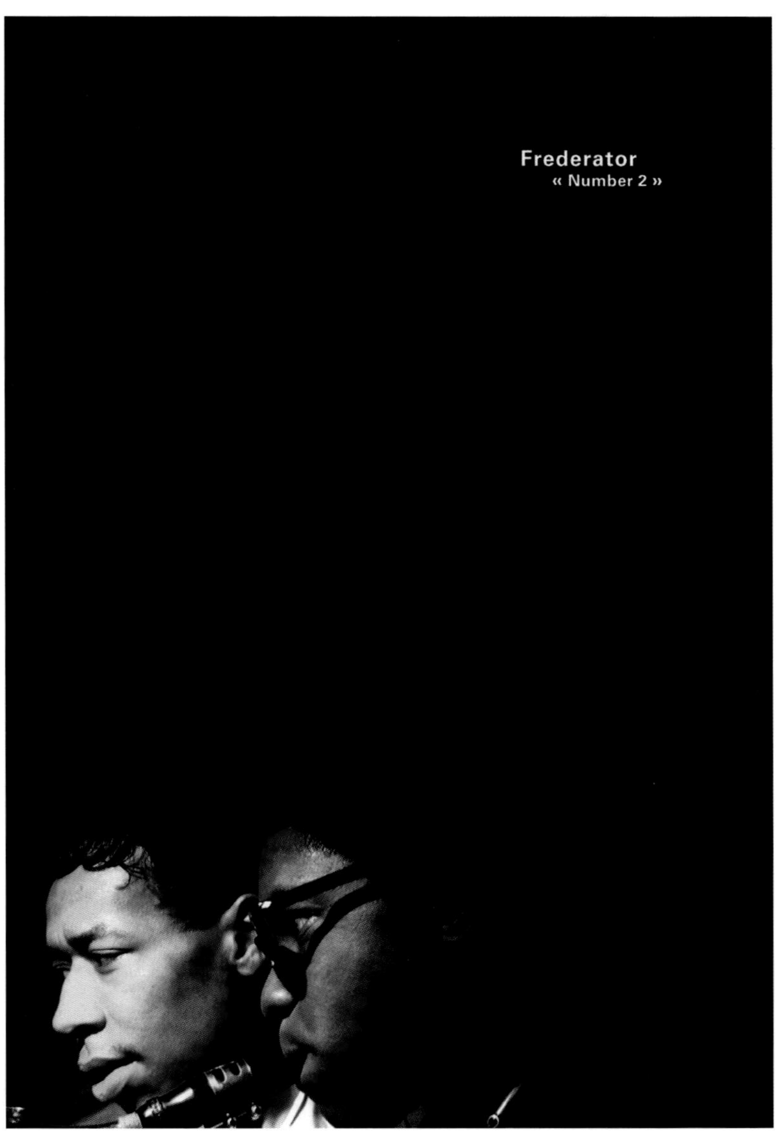

Design by AdamsMorioka
Photograph by Francis Wolff
Used with the kind permission of Mosiac Editions

FREDERATOR 3

```
startDrag ("/tracker", true, 150, 0, 450, 350); l = getProperty("/fred", _y)-
getProperty("/Centre", _y); g = 9.8; input = l/g; call ("sqrt"); t =
int((/:output*6.28318530718))/25; if (Number(/tracker/:press) == 0)
xpos = getProperty("/fred", _x); setProperty ("/fred", _x, Number(getProperty("/fred",_x))
+Number(xplus*(director/:motion))); xdisp = xpos-300; /:input = (l*l)-(xdisp*xdisp);
call ("sqrt"); ypos = /:output; setProperty ("/fred", _y, Number(ypos)+70);}
duplicateMovieClip ("line", "newLine1", 1); setProperty ("newLine1", _x,
getProperty("/centre", _x)); setProperty ("newLine1", _y, getProperty("/centre",
_y)); setProperty ("newLine1", _xscale, getProperty("/fred", _x)-
getProperty("/centre", _x)); setProperty ("newLine1", _yscale, getProperty("/fred",
_y)-getProperty("centre", _y)); hnow = 270-getProperty("/fred", _y); xplus =
(tracker/:amplitude)/(20*t)-(hnow/12); gotoAndPlay (_currentframe-1); n = 1;
counter = 0; while (Number(counter)<15) {n = n-((n*n-input)/(2*n)); counter =
Number(counter)+1;} /:output = n; if (Number(../tracker/:press) == 1) {if
(Number(getProperty("../fred", _x))>=300) {motion = -1;} else {motion = 1;}} if
(Number(../tracker/:press) == 0) {if ((Number(motion) == 1 and
umber(getProperty("../fred",
_x))>=Number(300+Number((../tracker/:amplitude)))) or (Number(motion) ==
Number(-1) and Number(getProperty("../fred", _x))<=Number(300-
(../tracker/:amplitude)))) {motion = -1*motion; if (Number(../tracker/:amplitude)>0)
../tracker/:amplitude = ../tracker/:amplitude-5; if (Number(../tracker/:amplitude)<0)
{../tracker/:amplitude = 0;} ../tracker/:h = 270-getProperty("../fred", _y); } else
{../tracker/:amplitude = 0; motion = 0;}}}
```

The fun postcard, enjoy.

Frederator #4

Design by AdamsMorioka

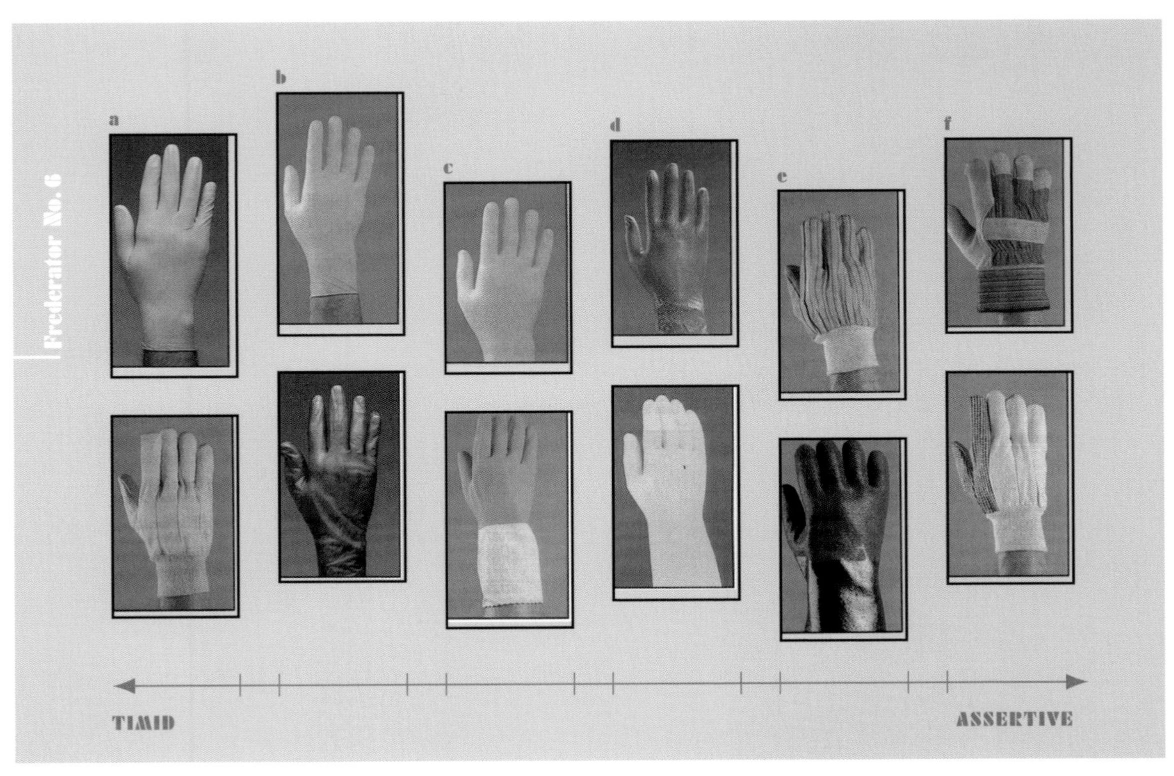

Design by AdamsMorioka

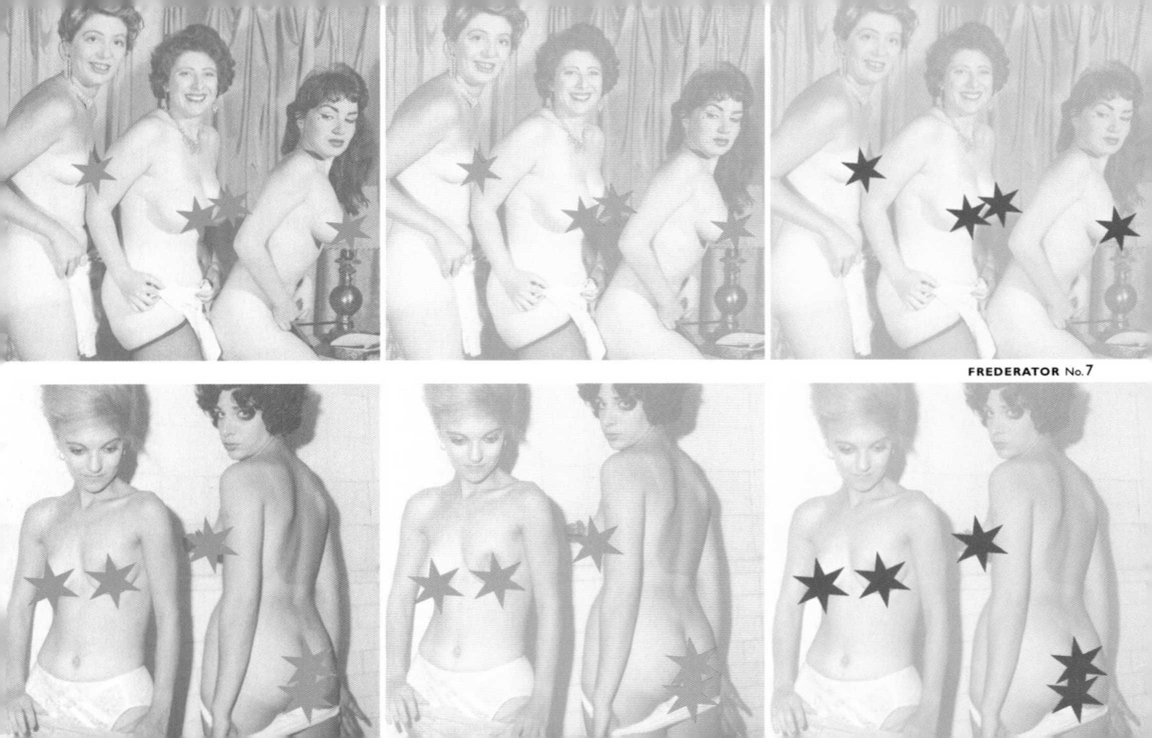

Design by AdamsMorioka

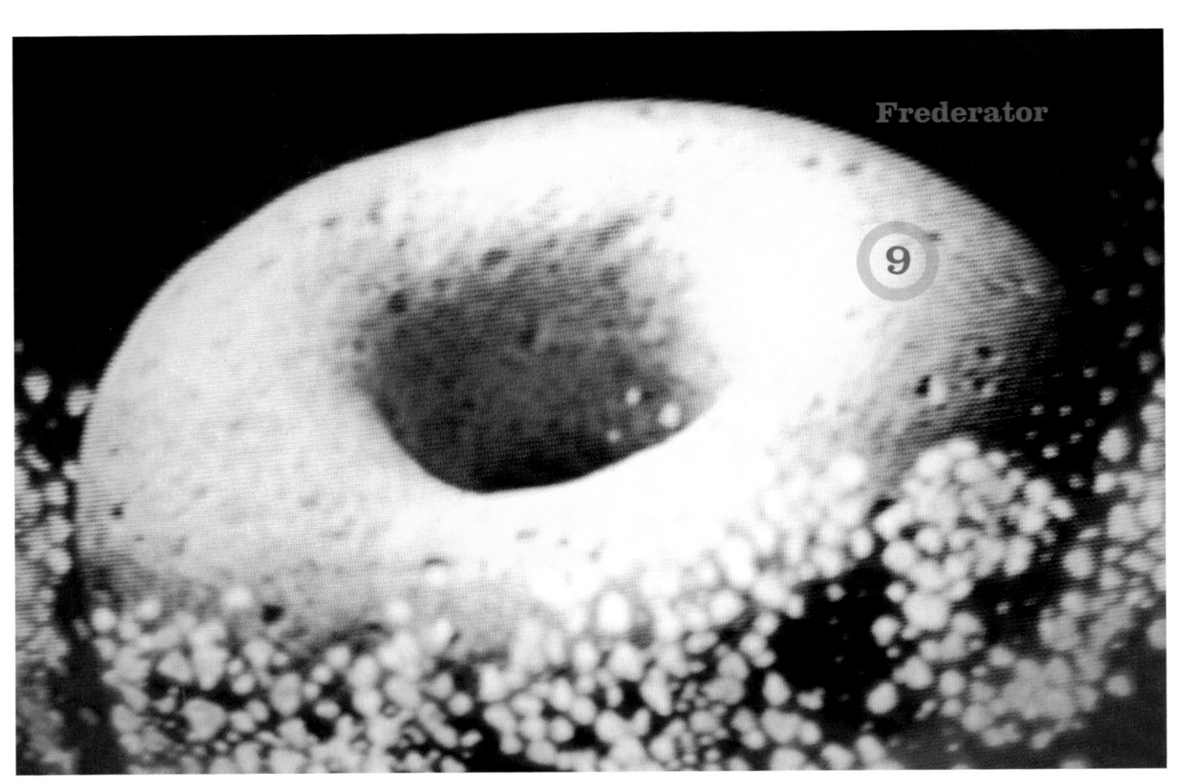

Design by AdamsMorioka

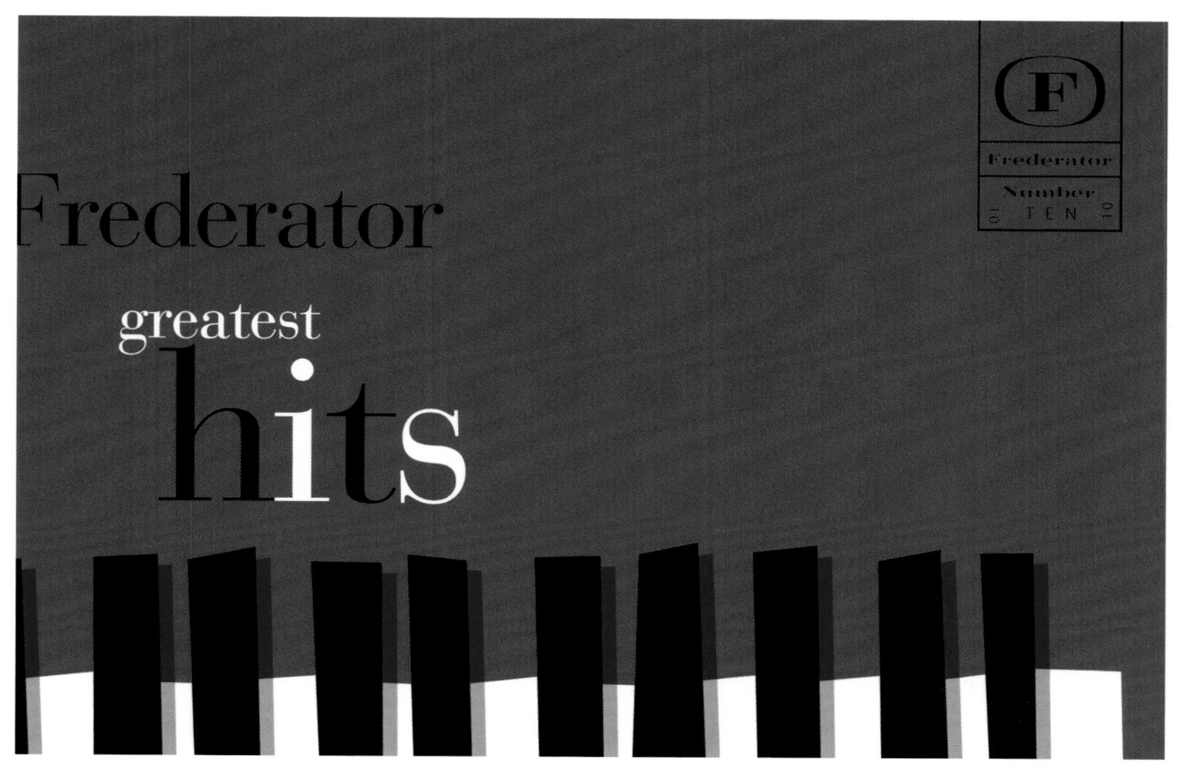

Design by AdamsMorioka

Design by AdamsMorioka

Design by AdamsMorioka

Design by AdamsMorioka

FREDERATOR No. 14

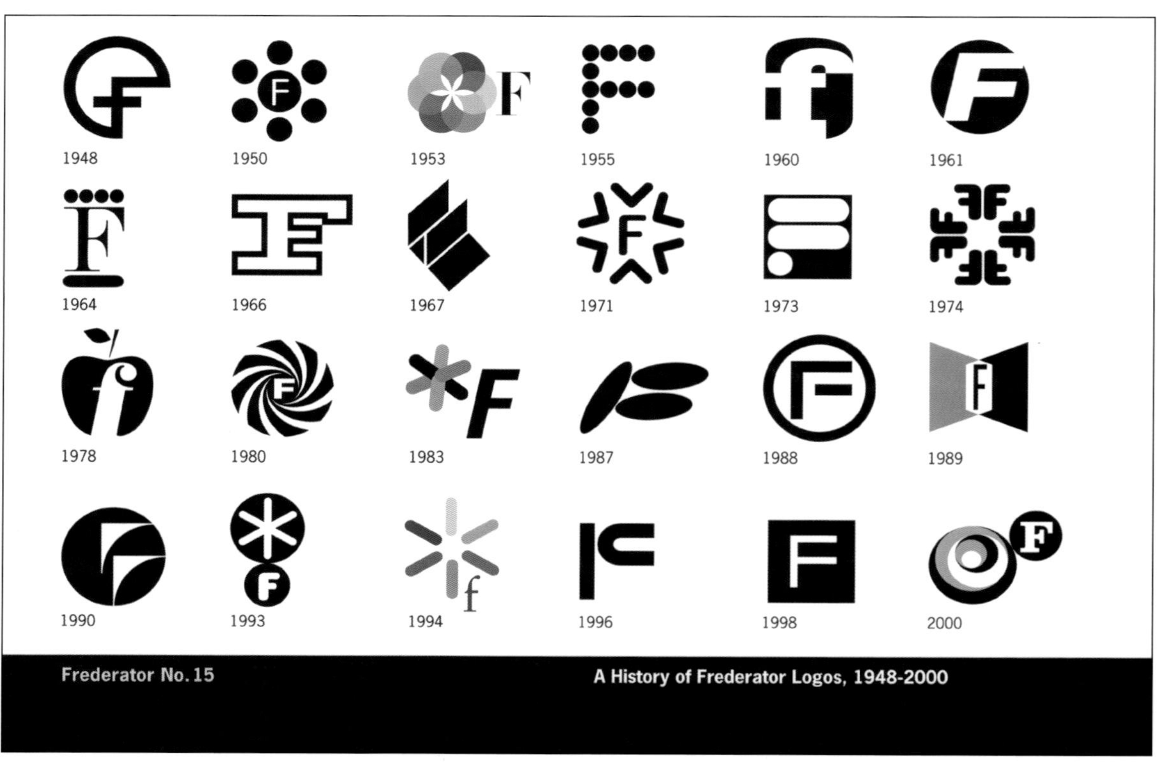

Design by AdamsMorioka

Design by AdamsMorioka

Design by AdamsMorioka

Design by AdamsMorioka

Fear of a horrible scandal and loss of a handsome fortune–these are the main actions involved in the necessity for the strange and warped actions of: Sandra Shaw–a 28 year-old hellion, also a step-mother; unbelievably beautiful, cunning, insanely and intensely vicious with only sex and murder on her mind. Marla Stewart–young, sensuous; yet with a strong desire for women and the sound of leather searing the soft flesh of those around her. Jim Bartlett–Sandra's stepson, naive, sensitive and frightened. Living in a house with two women, both diseased with corruption and immorality. His young mind and spirit weakened, almost destroyed by the female domination, discipline, and exposure to all types of perversions and depravity. Mrs. Adams–the next door neighbor, social threat, submissive target, and finally the victim. A frightening novel about those unknown, unspoken, abnormal desires and those who willingly submit to them. "You're crazy," she screamed. "You don't want Jim. He's downstairs. He killed her. I didn't have anything to do with it." "Nice try, Mrs. bartlett. You almost got away with it." "What are you talkin' about?" Smiling, Dick advanced toward her and forced her to back all the way into the living room where Marla, still wearing just bra and panties saw all the eyes of the men moving over her body. "Hello Jim," the detective greeted the boy as he walked into the room. "You did a great job. We have everything on tape." "Did you get enough?" "More than enough. While you were downstairs, they were discussing how to kill you, so that it would look like suicide." With a poised smile, Jim walked over to the table and picked up his watch. He handed it to the detective. "I guess you'll want your transmitter back. Thanks for the use of it. In fact, thanks for everything." "Don't mention it, Jim. You know, with this kind of training, maybe you'll decide to be a detective some day." "Maybe I will at that," the boy answered. The detectives took the two women in the bedroom to get dressed for the trip to the station. For a moment, Jim considered following for one last look at the two lush bodies. He changed his mind. After all, he reasoned, I've seen plenty of them. Let the cops enjoy a private show of their own. Jim suddenly felt very, very good. He was glad the detective told him the women planned to kill him, now he wouldn't have to bother feeling sorry for them. Roped Rendezvous by Myron Kosloff, 1968.

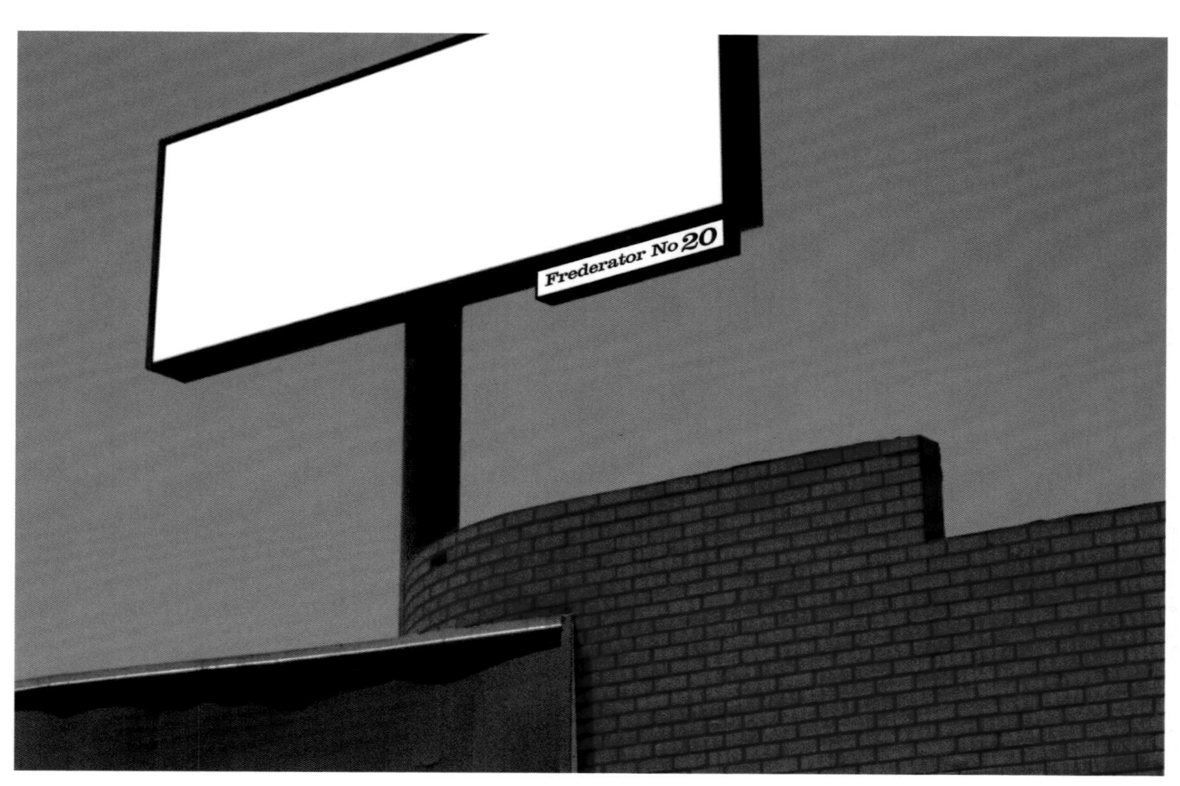

Design by AdamsMorioka

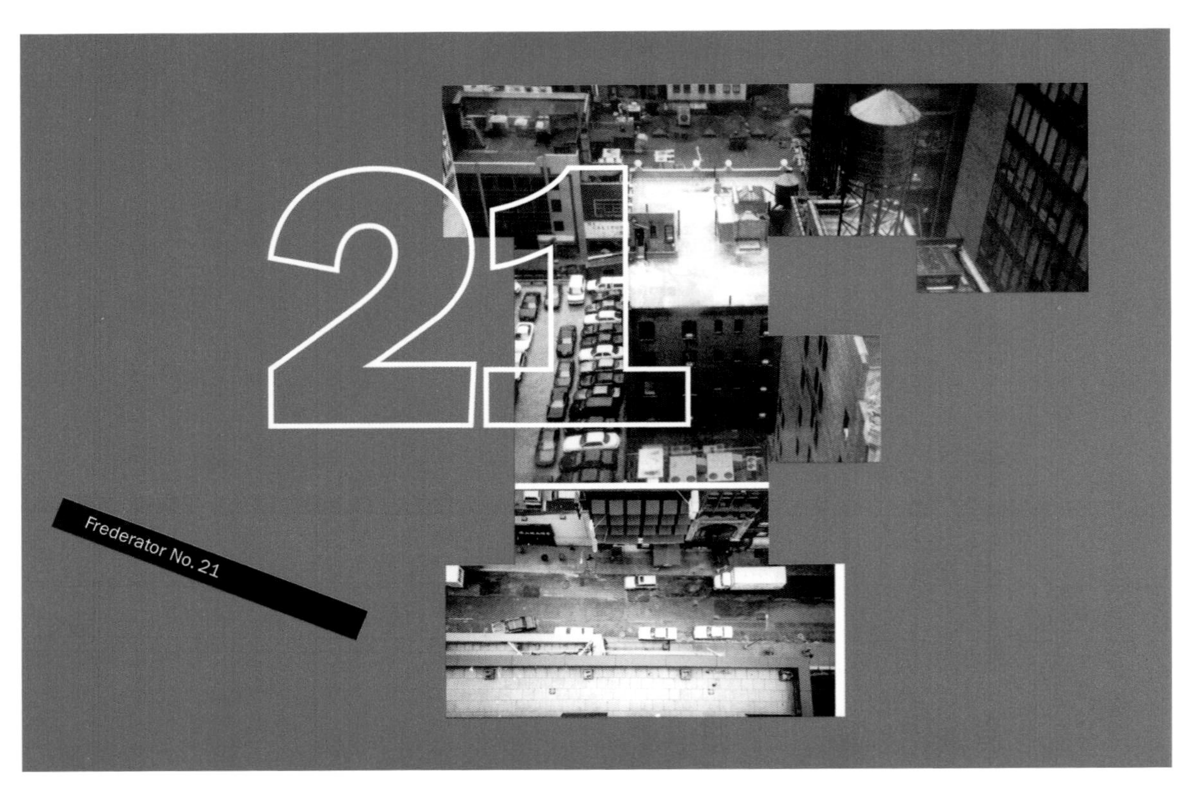

Design by AdamsMorioka

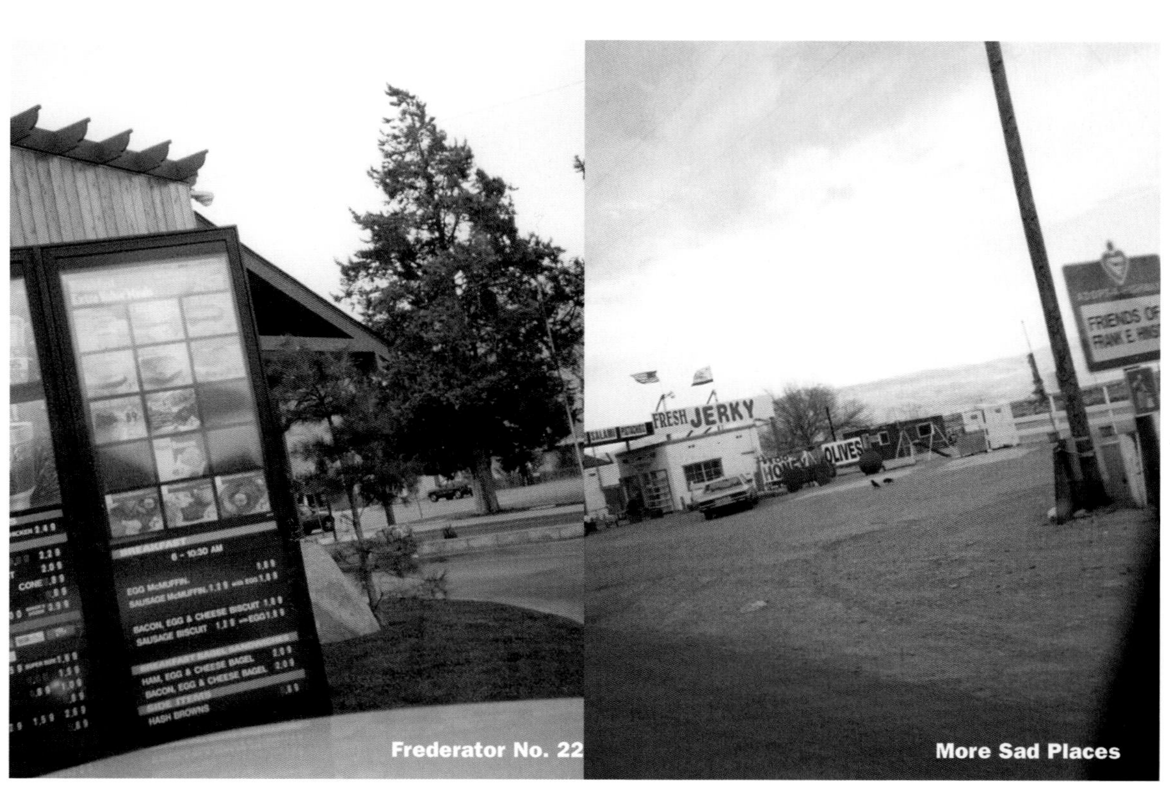

Frederator No. 22

More Sad Places

Design by AdamsMorioka

Frederator #23 Mexico City La Zona Rosa 1:30 p.m. 9.5.01

Design by AdamsMorioka

Postcard postcard

Frederator No. 24

Series 5 Postcards 2004 & 2005

Illustration by Eugene Mattos

Photograph courtesy of NASA
Illustration by Eugene Mattos

FREDERATOR STUDIOS

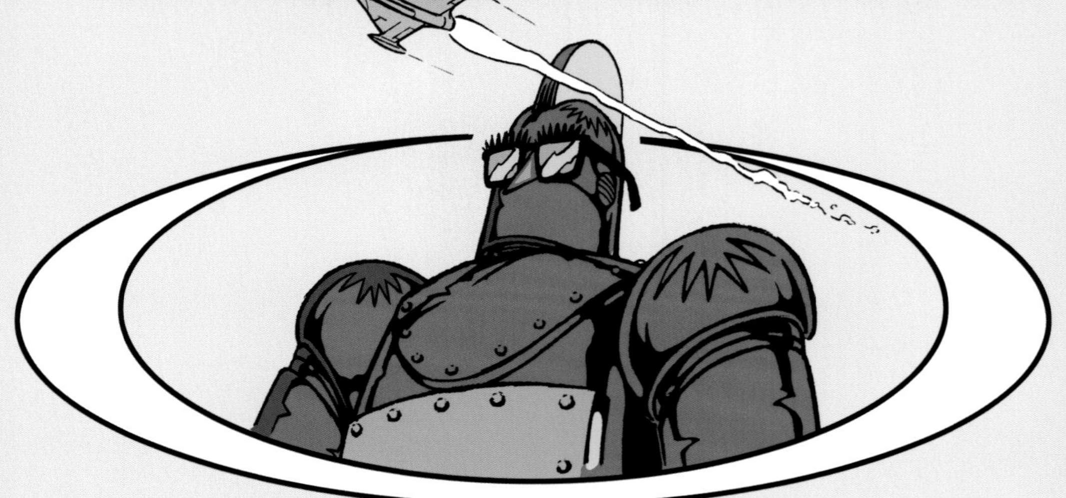

ORIGINAL CARTOONS SINCE 1998

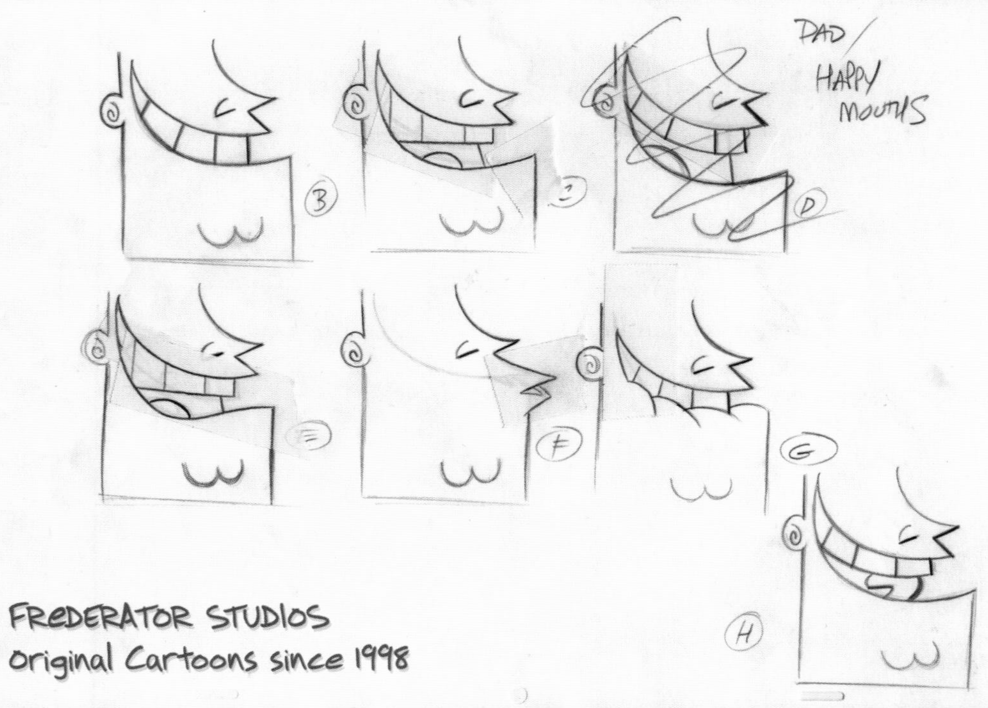

The Fairly Oddparents created by Butch Hartman

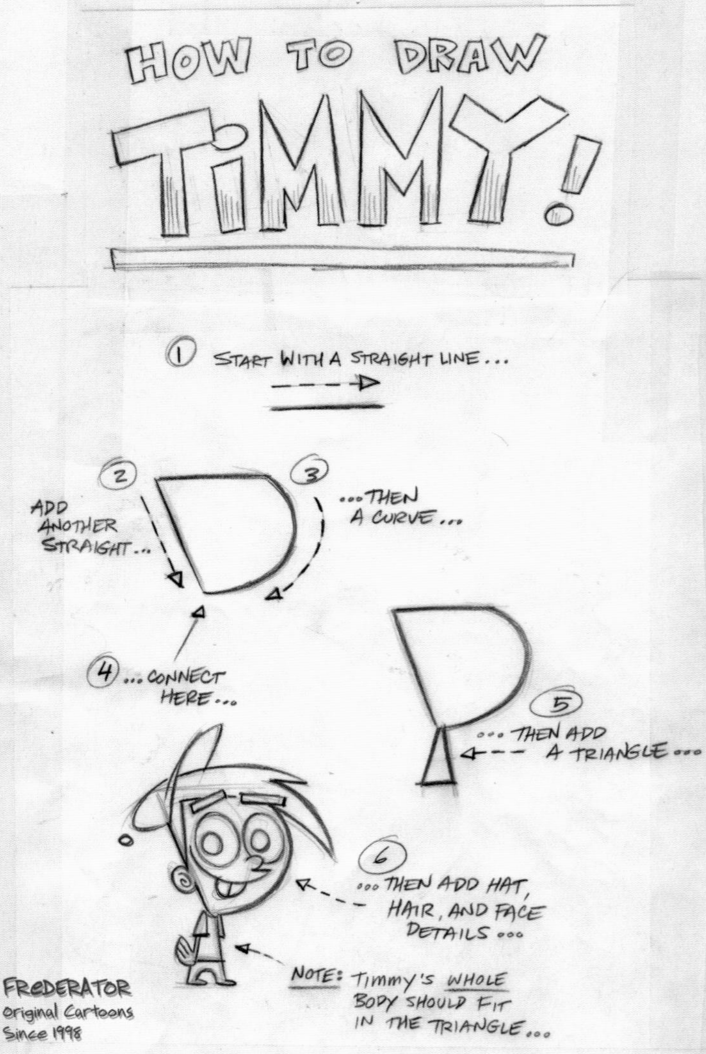

① START WITH A STRAIGHT LINE...

② ADD ANOTHER STRAIGHT...

③ ...THEN A CURVE...

④ ...CONNECT HERE...

⑤ ...THEN ADD A TRIANGLE...

⑥ ...THEN ADD HAT, HAIR, AND FACE DETAILS...

NOTE: Timmy's WHOLE BODY SHOULD FIT IN THE TRIANGLE...

FREDERATOR
Original Cartoons
Since 1998

CONTINUE HAIR CONTOUR AFTER HAIR BREAK
WHEN ANGRY, EYEBROWS EXTEND SLIGHTLY INTO HAIR MASS
THREE EYELASHES PER EYE!
EYES ON EACH SIDE OF FACE DIVISION LINE!
TINY BOOBS!
AFTER HAIR BREAK, CONTINUE HAIR CONTOUR!
LIPS ARE SLIGHTLY OFFSET, AND TO ONE SIDE OF FACE DIVISION LINE!
ANGULAR ELBOWS!
A SIMPLE "6" SWIRL IN THE EAR
DON'T FORGET THE BELLY BUTTON!
KEEP EYES INSIDE OF FACE SHAPE!
SMALL TORSO!
THIS IS RIGHT!
FEET ARE VERY SIMPLE!
LEGS TAPER TO FEET!
THIS IS WRONG!
HANDS ARE A SIMPLE SHAPE!
KEEP MOUTH INSIDE FACE SHAPE!
THIS IS RIGHT!
THIS IS WRONG!

FREDERATOR STUDIOS: Original cartoons since 1998

the Fairly OddParents!

#133"FOOL'S DAY OUT"

CHARACTER

scene:

same as:

FREDERATOR STUDIOS

ORIGINAL CARTOONS SINCE 1998

1. OH YEAH! CARTOONS
(Fred Seibert, 1998)
2. THE FAIRLY ODDPARENTS
(Butch Hartman, 2000)
3. CHALKZONE
(Bill Burnett & Larry Huber, 2002)
Original Cartoons
since 1998
FREDERATOR
STUDIOS
2
4. MY LIFE AS A TEENAGE ROBOT
(Rob Renzetti, 2003)
od.4.stereo

FREDERATOR
Original cartoons since 1998
produced with Nickeldeon
HITS!
My Life as a Teenage Robot
The Farily Oddparents
Oh Yeah! Cartoons
ChalkZone

MADE IN U.S.A.
FULL-RANGE
RECORDING
Vocalion
Fox Trot
(E 36212)
Vocal Chorus
FREDERATOR STUDIOS
(New York City)
(and)
-Burbank-
ORIGINAL CARTOONS
since 1998
4753

Red Bird
Tender Toons
Films, Inc.
Trio Music Co.,
Inc.-BMI
A Seibert-Sloane
Production
RB 10-014
L /S 1041
Time: 2:55
FREDERATOR STUDIOS
(New York, Burbank)
ORIGINAL CARTOONS
SINCE 1998

BANG
CARTOONS
Robert Mellin, Inc.
Picturetone Music
Pub. Corp.--- BMI
W-10013
Time: 2:57
FREDERATOR STUDIOS
(New York and Burbank)
ORIGINAL CARTOONS SINCE 1998
Arranged and Conducted by Bassett Hand
A Seibert & Sloane
Production
B-506

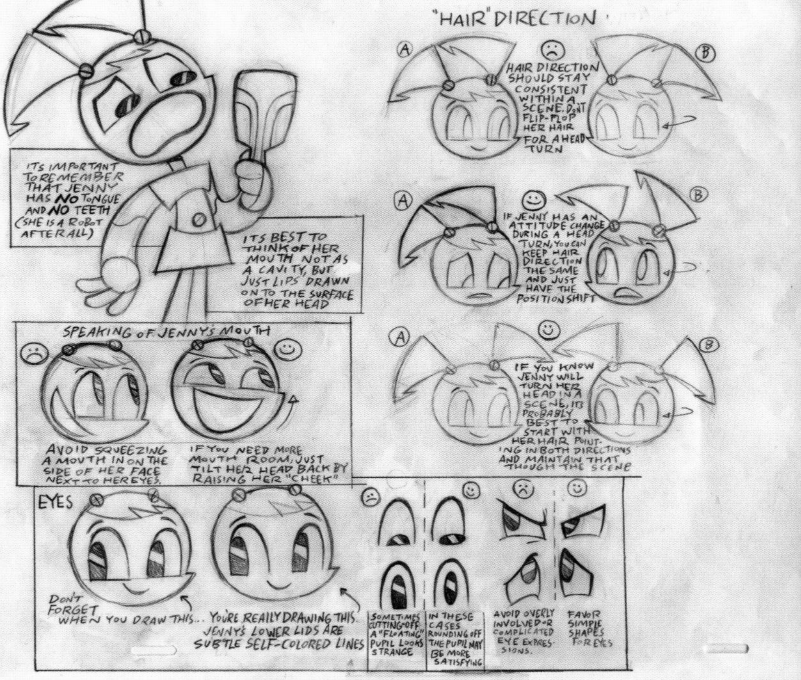

My Life as a Teenage Robot created by Rob Renzetti

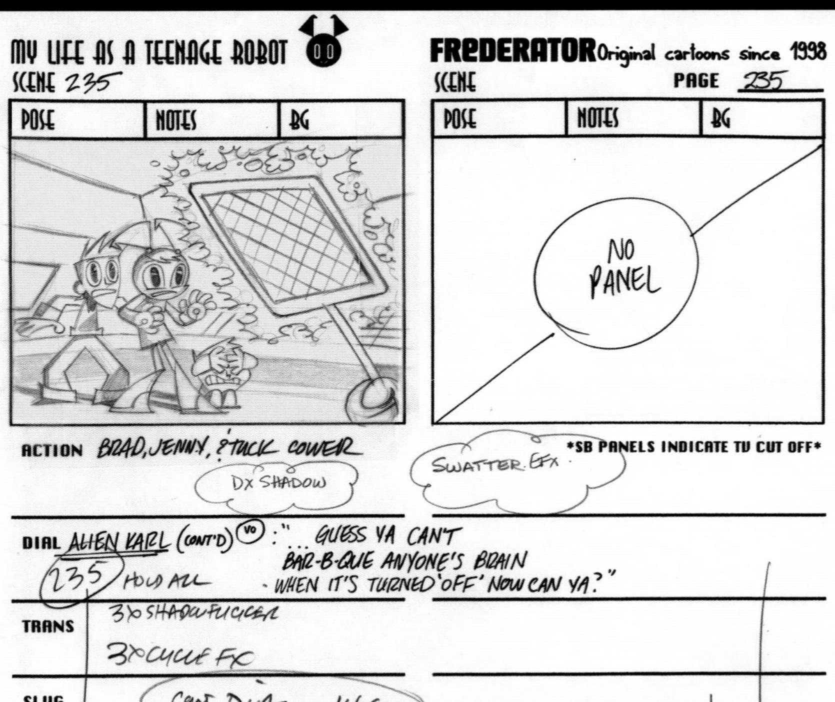

MY LIFE AS A TEENAGE ROBOT
SCENE 235
FREDERATOR Original cartoons since 1998
SCENE
PAGE 235
POSE
NOTES
BG
POSE
NOTES
BG
NO PANEL
ACTION BRAD, JENNY, & TUCK COWER
DX SHADOW
SWATTER EFX
SB PANELS INDICATE TV CUT OFF
DIAL ALIEN KARL (CONT'D) (VO): "... GUESS YA CAN'T BAR-B-QUE ANYONE'S BRAIN WHEN IT'S TURNED 'OFF' NOW CAN YA?"
235 HOLD ALL
TRANS 3X SHADOW FLICKER
3X CYCLE FX
SLUG CONT. DIAL 146

My Life as a Teenage Robot created by Rob Renzetti

FREDERATOR STUDIOS
ORIGINAL CARTOONS SINCE 1998

NICKELODEON
MY LIFE AS A
TEENAGE ROBOT™

My Life as a Teenage Robot created by Rob Renzetti

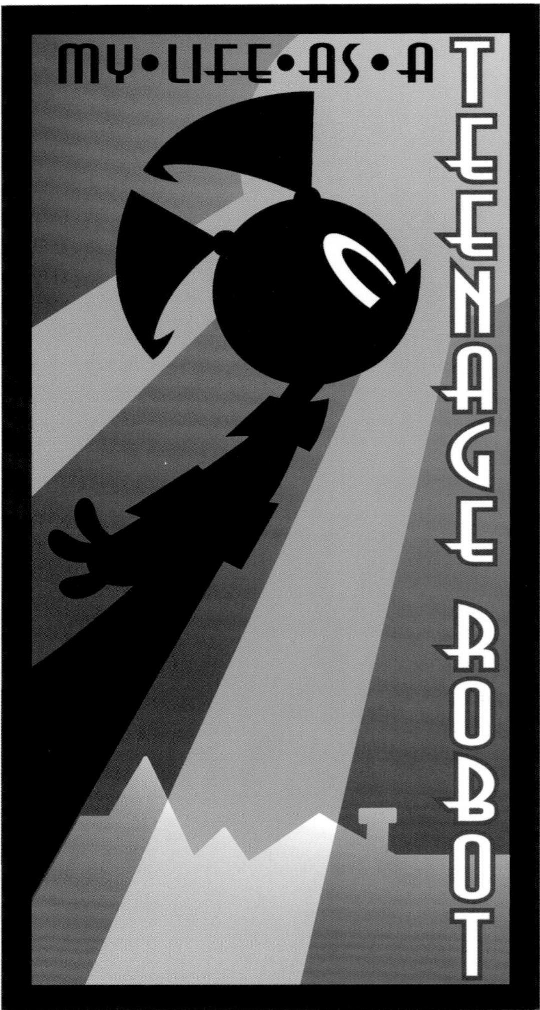

FREDERATOR STUDIOS
ORIGINAL CARTOONS SINCE 1998

My Life as a Teenage Robot created by Rob Renzetti
Illustration by Jill Friemark

My Life as a Teenage Robot created by Rob Renzetti

ChalkZone created by Bill Burnett & Larry Huber

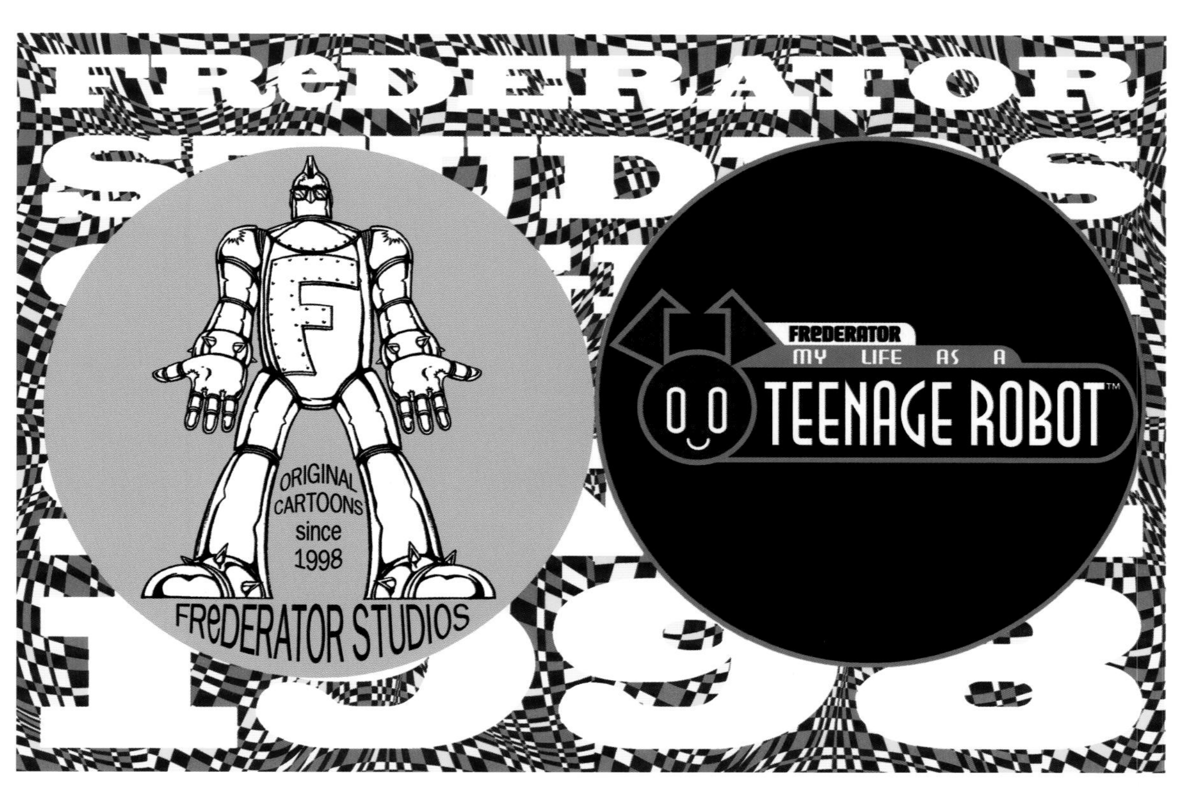

My Life as a Teenage Robot created by Rob Renzetti

The Fairly Oddparents created by Butch Hartman

ORIGINAL CARTOONS 1998
38
37
FRED
CENTS
2004
ORIGINAL CARTOONS 1998
37
37
FRED
CENTS
2004
UNITED STATES POSTAGE
ORIGINAL CARTOONS SINCE 1998
2004
37
1804
CARTOON HERITAGE MONTH
37
USA
The Fairly Oddparents
USA
23
Cosmo
2004
2¢
USA
CHALKZONE 2004
TEENAGE
ROBOT
32 USA 2004
Original Cartoons
since 1998
USA
29
FRED SEIBERT

FREDERATOR STUDIOS' HIT SERIES

Oh Yeah! Cartoons

"Created by Fred Seibert"

ChalkZone

"Created by Bill Burnett & Larry Huber"

CARTOONS since 1998

The Fairly Oddparents

"Created by Butch Hartman"

My Life as a Teenage Robot

"Created by Rob Renzetti"

ON THE NICKELODEON NETWORKS

ORIGINAL CARTOONS SINCE 1998

WANTED

FReDERATOR

No. 958039BEF

Photo taken circa 1977

R. Thumb	R. Index	R. Middle	R. Ring	R.Little
L. Little	L. Ring	L. Middle	L. Index	L. Thumb

DESCRIPTION

AGE: 52 born September 15, 1951, New York, New York
HEIGHT: 6' 2"

WEIGHT: too much	EYES: blue
BUILD: formerly narrow	COMPLEXION:
HAIR: brown	RACE: slow
SCARS AND MARKS: right wrist	NATIONALITY: American
	ALIASES: Bone

CAUTION

FREDERATOR X. FREDERATOR, A SELF PROCLAIMED MEMBER OF THE CARTOON LIBERATION ARMY REPORTEDLY HAS BEEN IN POSSESSION OF NUMEROUS TOOLS, INCLUDING APPLE G4 COMPUTERS, LOADED WITH SCRIPTS AND STORYBOARDS FROM THE FAIRLY ODDPARENTS, CHALKZONE, MY LIFE AS A TEENAGE ROBOT, AOL INSTANT MESSENGER, AND LIME WIRE, A PROVEN P2P FILE SHARING VIOLATOR, ENEMY OF THE MUSIC AND FILMS INDUSTRIES ALIKE.

A Federal warrent was issued on May 29, 2003 in Los Angeles, California, charging Frederator X. Frederator with violation of the National Cartooning Act (U.S. Code 59632) on January 1, 1998 \in New York City, New York State released by a Federal Grand Jury, in Kings County, New York, New York (Title 19, U.S. Code Securities 012430).

IF YOUR HAVE INFORMATION CONCERNING THIS PERSON, PLEASE CONTACT YOUR LOCAL FBI OFFICE. TELEPHONE NUMBERS AND ADDRESSES OF ALL OFFICES LISTED ON BACK.

Identification Codes 3993

Director
Federal Cartoons Bureau
Washington D.C. 02203

FREDERATOR
STUDIOS
ORIGINAL CARTOONS
SINCE 1998

Original
Cartoons
Since
1998
FREDERATOR
STUDIOS
©arlos ®amos

oh
yeah
CARTOONS
FREDERATOR
ORIGINAL CARTOONS SINCE 1998

FREDERATOR
STUDIOS
ORIGINAL
SINCE
1998
CARTOONS
OH YEAH!

Mom & DAD AT ORIGINAL HARBOR PHARMACY, Huntington NY

FREDERATOR STUDIOS - ORIGINAL CARTOONS SINCE 1998

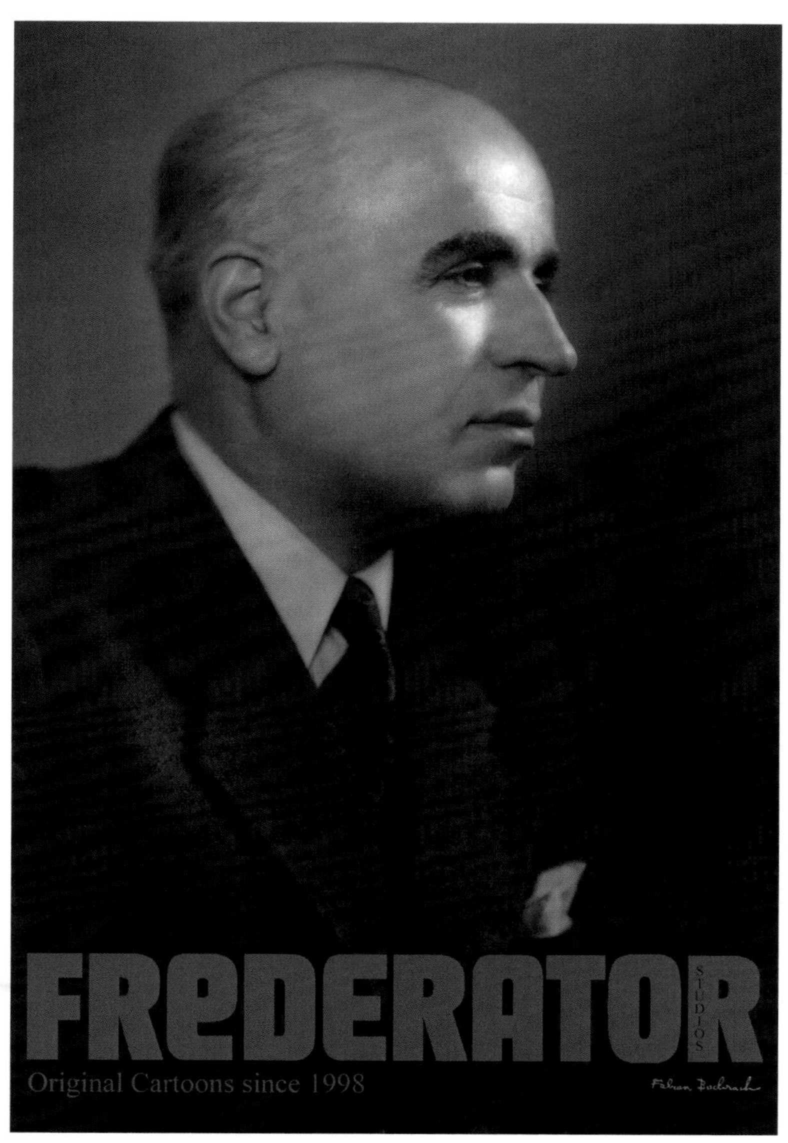

Photograph by Fabian Bachrach

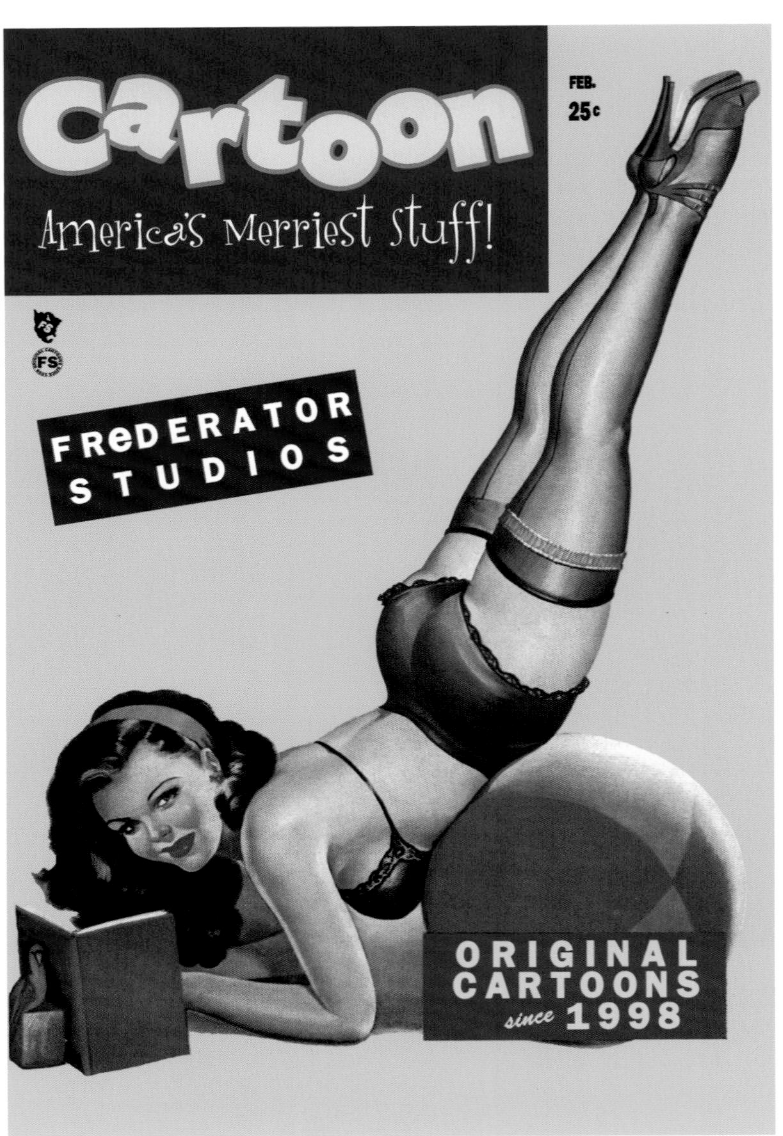
Cartoon
FEB.
25c
America's Merriest Stuff!
FREDERATOR
STUDIOS
ORIGINAL
CARTOONS
since 1998

FREDERATOR STUDIOS
Original Cartoons since 1998
COLLECTOR'S CARD
$225
WATCH OUR HITS!
The
Fairly Oddparents
CHALKZONE
My Life as a
Teenage Robot
OH YEAH!
CARTOONS
Hundreds more!

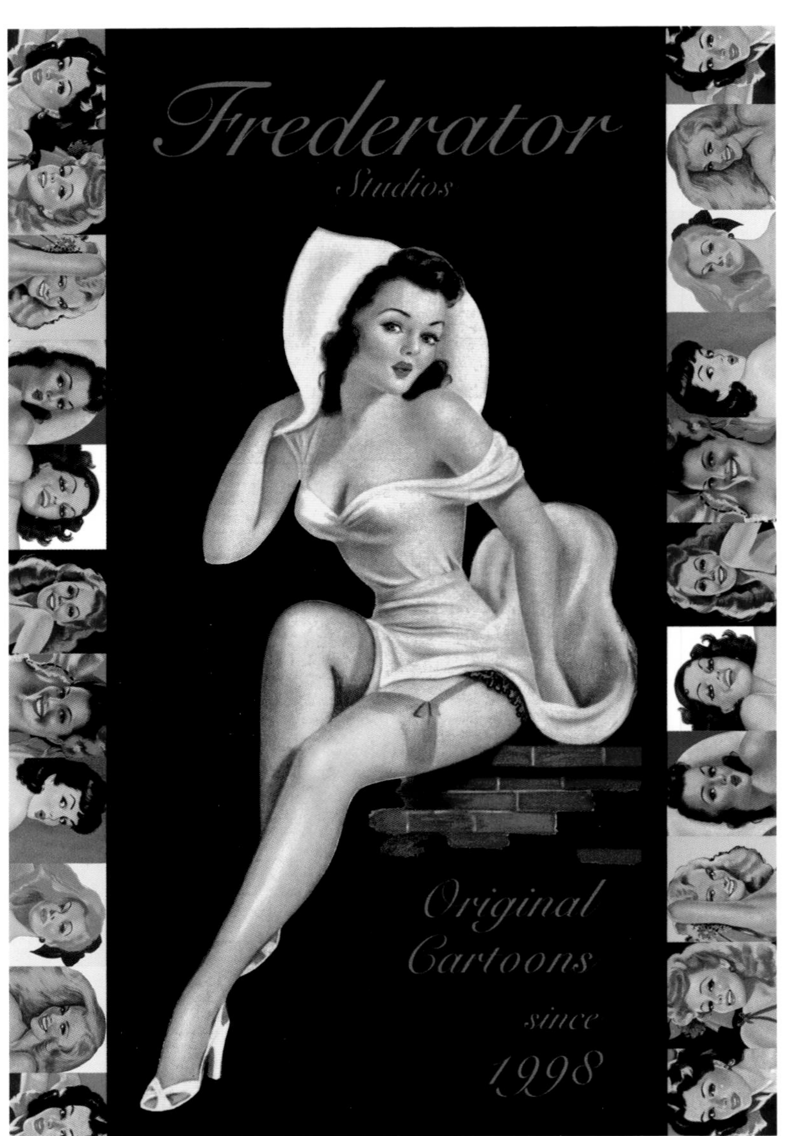
Frederator
Studios
Original
Cartoons
since
1998

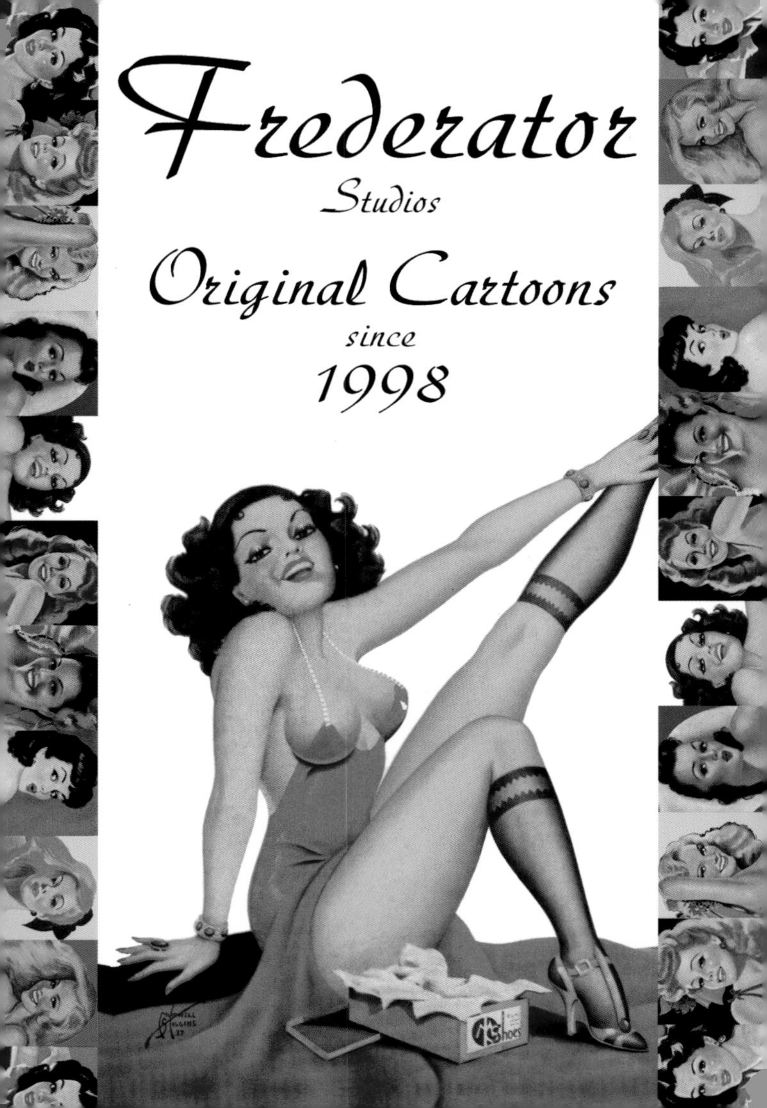
Frederator
Studios
Original Cartoons
since
1998

FREDERATOR
STUDIOS
ORIGINAL CARTOONS
SINCE 1998

FREDERATOR STUDIOS
ORIGINAL CARTOONS SINCE 1998

CHALKZONE

ChalkQueen

an 11-minute script

by
Larry Huber

First Draft: 2/04/03
Please respond with notes by: 2/06/03

CC: Bill Burnett, Tanya Calderon, Marjorie Cohn, Debby Hindman, Dean Hoff, Larry Huber, George Lentino, Melissa Lugar, Rich Magallanes, Jenny Nissenson, Jennie Monica, Erica Ottenberg, Courtney Sanford, Peggy Sarlin, Mark Taylor, Aydrea Walden

Nickelodeon Animation Studios

Frederator Studios: Original Cartoons since 1998

ChalkZone created by Bill Burnett & Larry Huber

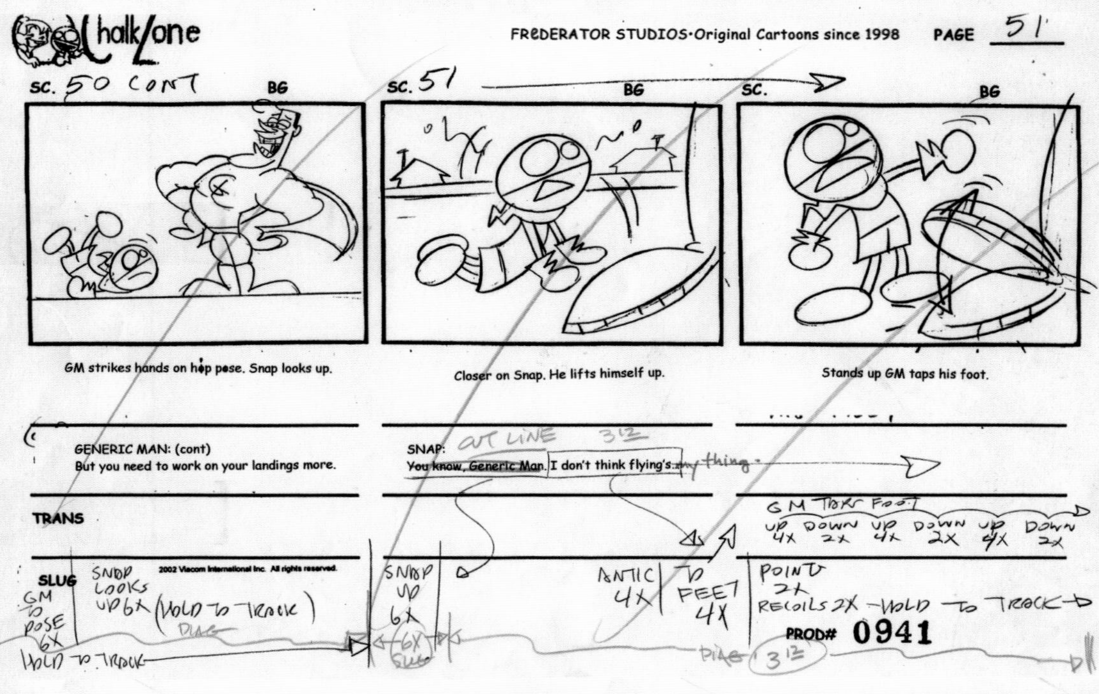
ChalkZone
FREDERATOR STUDIOS·Original Cartoons since 1998
PAGE 51
SC. 50 CONT
BG
SC. 51
BG
SC.
BG
GM strikes hands on hip pose. Snap looks up.
Closer on Snap. He lifts himself up.
Stands up GM taps his foot.
GENERIC MAN: (cont)
But you need to work on your landings more.
SNAP:
You know, Generic Man. I don't think flying's my thing.
TRANS
SLUG
2002 Viacom International Inc. All rights reserved.
PROD# 0941

ORIGINAL CARTOONS SINCE 1998
FREDERATOR
STUDIOS

HI SCOTT —
HE (SNAP)
CAN NOT BE
SHADED (FOR
COLOR REASONS)
FRIED
SNAP
SC-55
OK
10/30/02
CLEAN-UP WORK
DONE 11-13-02

ChalkZone created by Bill Burnett & Larry Huber

MAIN MODEL

SHOW #:

SCENE:

CHARACTER

DESIGN #
6

Location: REAL WORLD 5/8/2003

RUDY TABOOTIE
NORMAL MOUTH CHART

INS. MOUTH - 161/57/57
TOOTH - 237/239/233
TONGUE - 221/137/137

FOR MOUTH REFERENCE ONLY

FREDERATOR STUDIOS

ORIGINAL CARTOONS SINCE 1998

ChalkZone created by Bill Burnett & Larry Huber
Painting by Frank Rocco

Coming in 2005

BOLDER MEDIA from

Mixed Media Group

+ Frederator

Present for the first time ever!

Books & Television Series for Preschool kids

LOTS OF CREATORS

50 ORIGINAL CHARACTERS

MORE ORIGINAL CARTOONS

Frederator Studios

Original Cartoons since 1998

FREDERATOR STUDIOS &
MIXED MEDIA GROUP PRESENT

BOLDER
BOOKS & CARTOONS
MEDIA

FREDERATOR. CARTOONS SINCE 1998

BOLDER MEDIA from the Mixed Media Group and FREDERATOR Studios

BOOKS & CARTOONS FOR PRE-SCHOOLERS

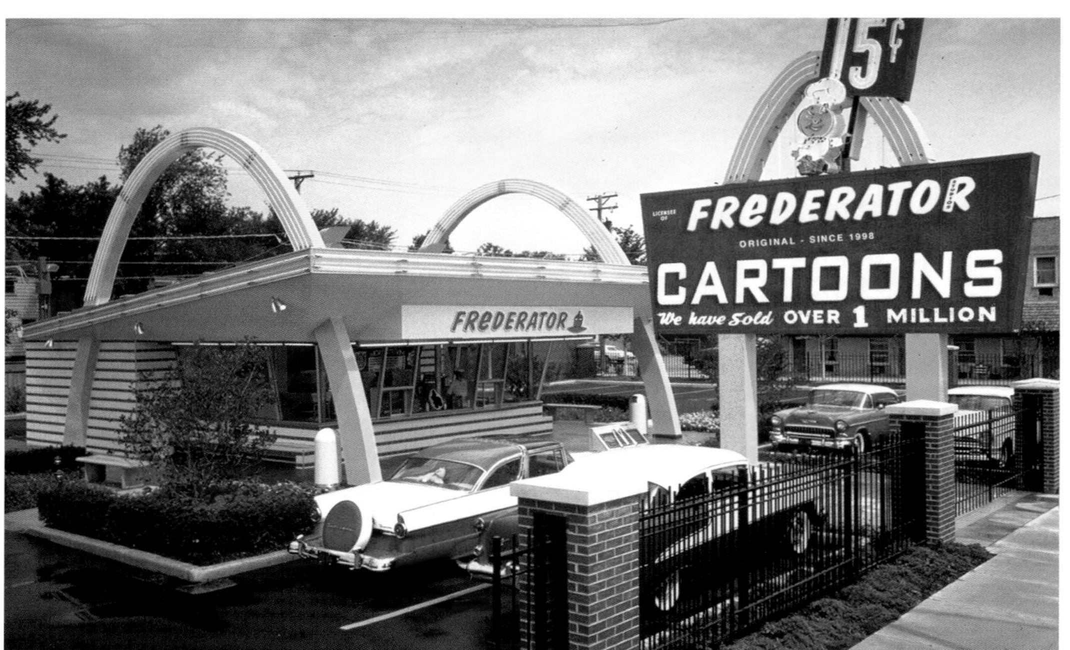
15¢
FREDERATOR
ORIGINAL - SINCE 1998
CARTOONS
We have Sold OVER 1 MILLION
FREDERATOR

Frederator Studios

Original Cartoons since 1998

Ha!

FREDERATOR STUDIOS

ORIGINAL CARTOONS SINCE 1998

HA!

FREDERATOR STUDIOS

ORIGINAL CARTOONS SINCE 1998

FREDERATOR STUDIOS

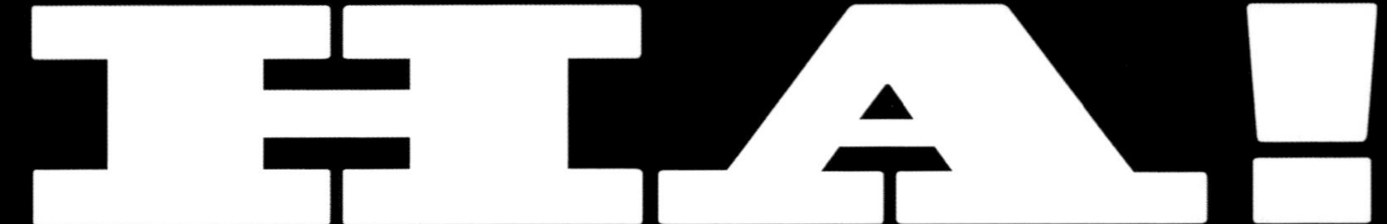

ORIGINAL CARTOONS SINCE 1998

Painting by Sam Steinberg

Painting by Jorge R. Gutierrez

Illustration: background from *Super Secret Secret Squirrel*

Painting by Miles Thompson

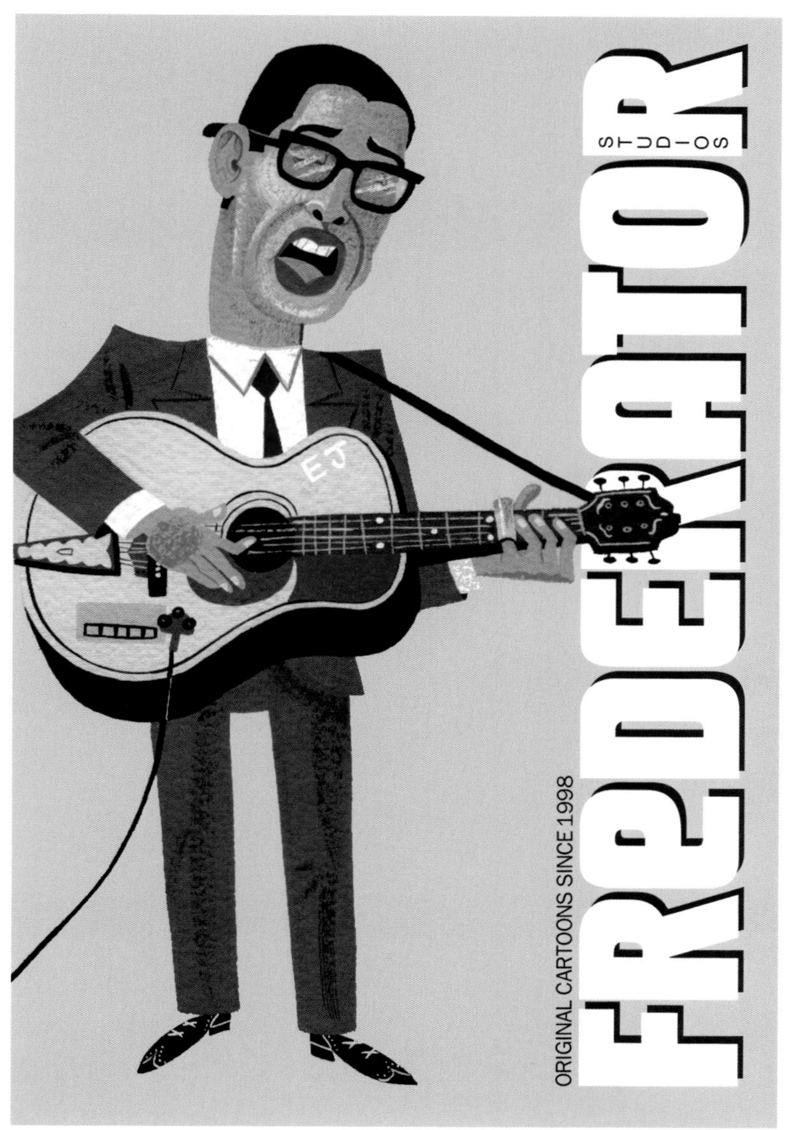

Painting by Miles Thompson

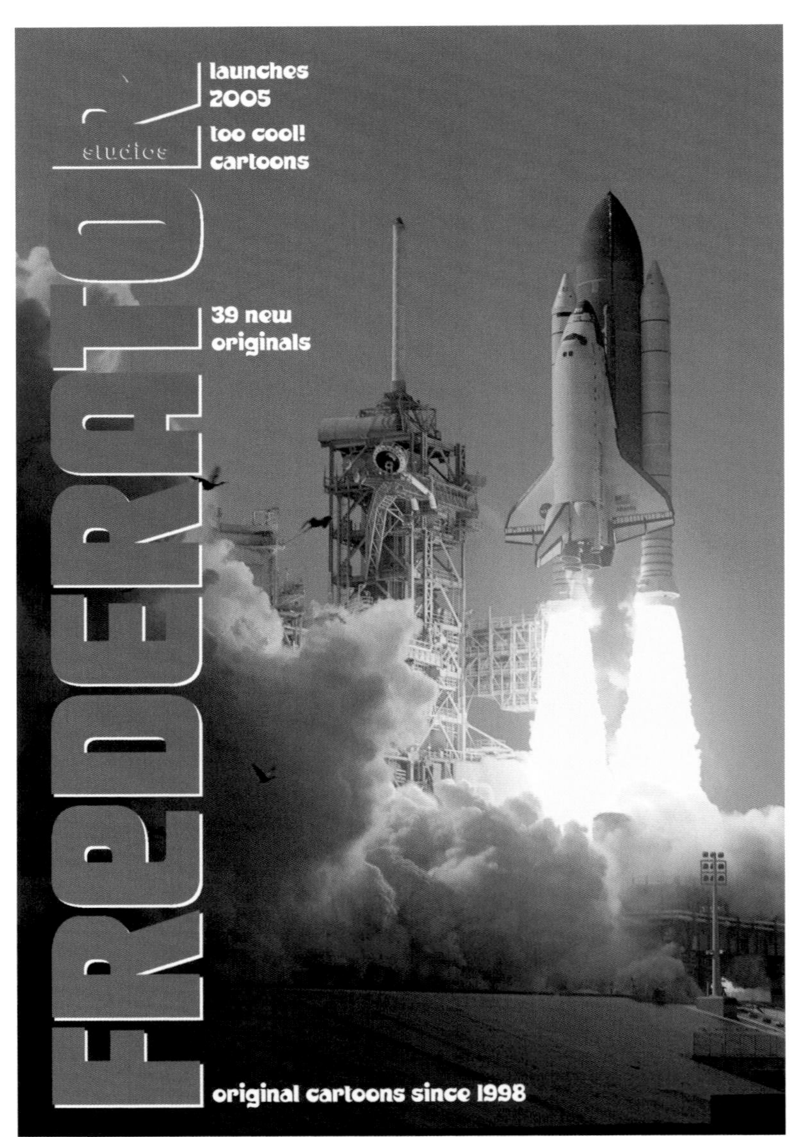

Photograph courtesy of NASA

Photograph courtesy of NASA

39 NEW SHORTS
TOO COOL! CARTOONS
FREDERATOR
ORIGINAL CARTOONS SINCE 1998

Photograph courtesy of NASA

FREDERATOR
STUDIOS
ORIGINAL CARTOONS SINCE
19
98

Illustration by CSA Images

ORIGINAL CARTOONS SINCE 1998

FREDERATOR STUDIOS

IN PRODUCTION 2004

FREDERATOR STUDIOS

TOO COOL! CARTOONS!

39 MORE ORIGINAL CARTOONS

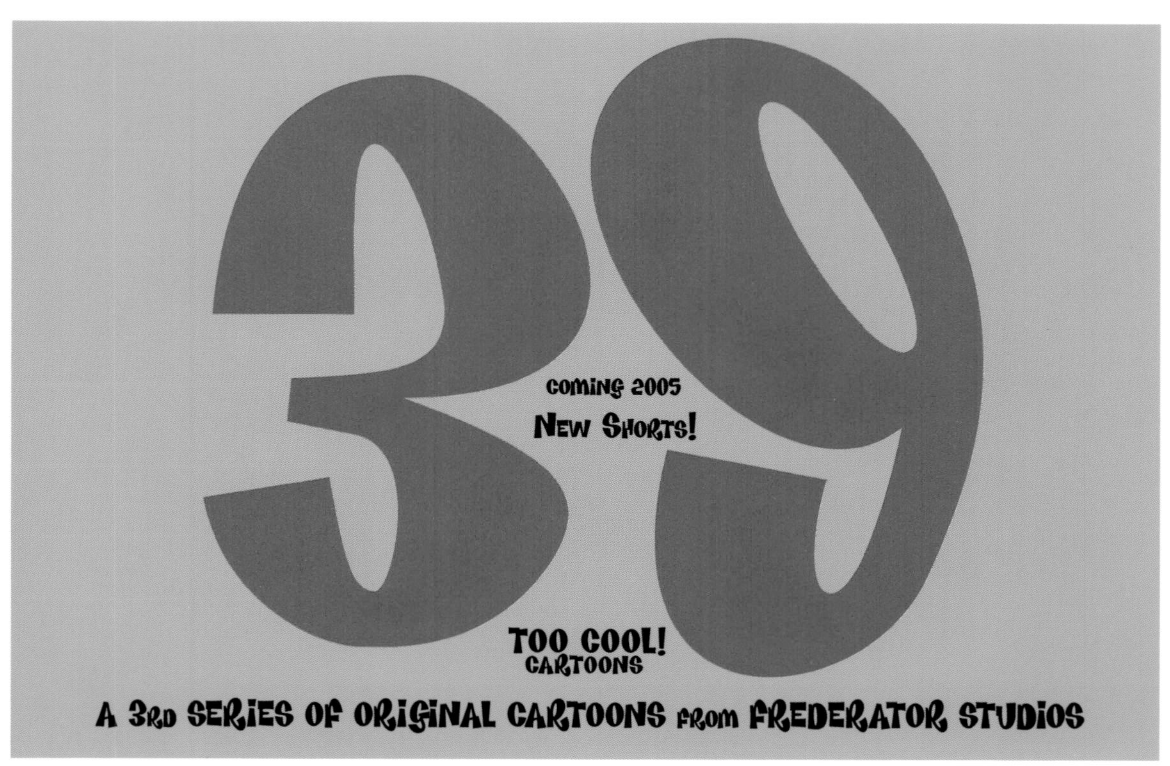
39
COMING 2005
NEW SHORTS!
TOO COOL!
CARTOONS
A 3RD SERIES OF ORIGINAL CARTOONS FROM FREDERATOR STUDIOS

FREDERATOR

Studios.

noun plural stu·di·os
An artist's workroom. A photographer's establishment.
An establishment where an art is taught or studied: a dance studio.
A room, building, or group of buildings where cartoons, movies, television shows, or radio programs are produced.
A room or building where tapes and records are produced.
A company that produces cartoons or films. A studio apartment.

Original

noun
A person who is appealingly odd or curious; a character.
The source from which something arises; an originator.
A first form from which other forms are made or developed:
Later models of the cartoon retained many features of the original.
An authentic work of art: bought an original, not a print.
Work that has been composed firsthand:
kept the original but sent a photocopy to his publisher.
Archaic.

Cartoons

noun
An animated cartoon. A comic strip.
A ridiculously oversimplified or stereotypical representation.
A drawing depicting a humorous situation, often accompanied by a caption.
A drawing representing current public figures or issues symbolically and often satirically: a political cartoon.
A preliminary sketch similar in size to the work that is to be copied from it.

since 1998.

COMING 2005
TOO COOL! CARTOONS! 39 MORE SHORTS!
FREDERATOR
SHORT CARTOONS
(SERIES 3)
LOTS OF CREATORS
NEW CHARACTERS
MORE CARTOONS
FREDERATOR STUDIOS
ORIGINAL CARTOONS SINCE 1998

A Frederator Studios Reminder

Election Day, November 2, 2004

A FREDERATOR STUDIOS REMINDER

ELECTION DAY, NOVEMBER 2, 2004

Election Day, November 2, 2004

frederator studios
original cartoons since 1998
& I care about this why?

FREDERATOR STUDIOS
ORIGINAL CARTOONS SINCE 1998

What does this have to do with me?

This sandwich is strange.

Hello.
FREDERATOR STUDIOS
Original Cartoons since 1998
Do we get a line?

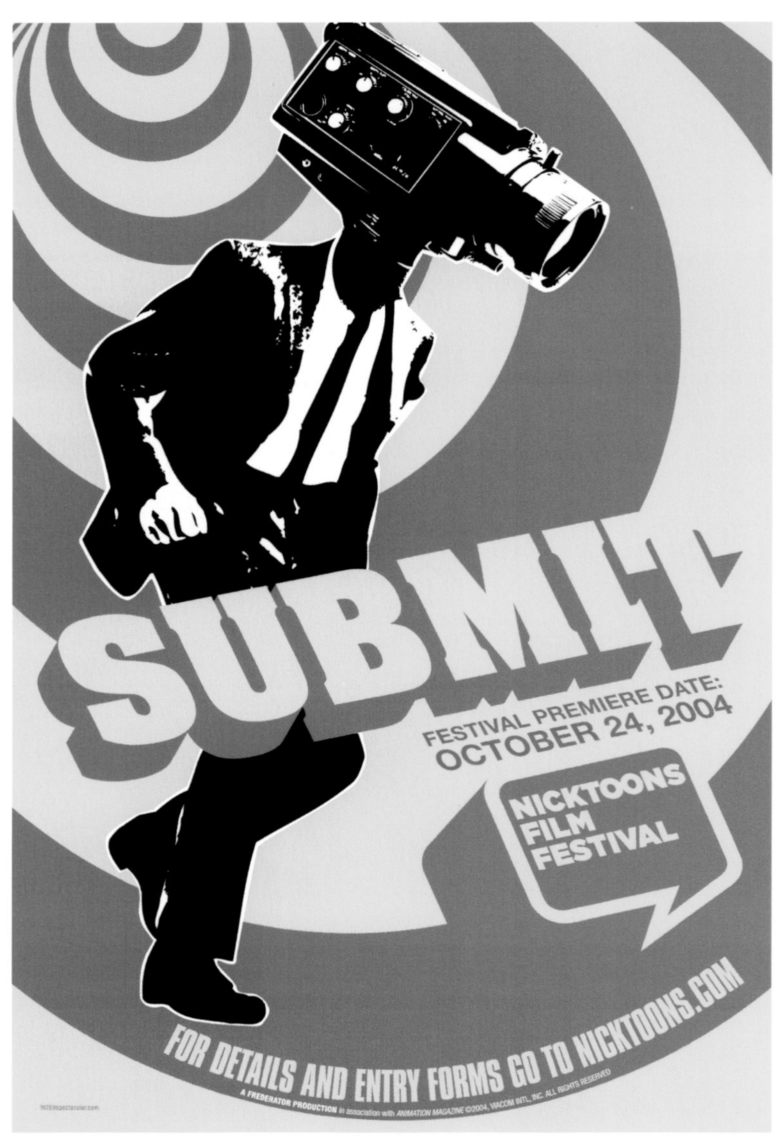

Design by INTERspectacular

Logo design by INTERspectacula

NICKTOONS FILM FESTIVAL

PREMIERING
October 24, 2004

A FREDERATOR PRODUCTION
in association with ANIMATION MAGAZINE

Posters 1994-2004

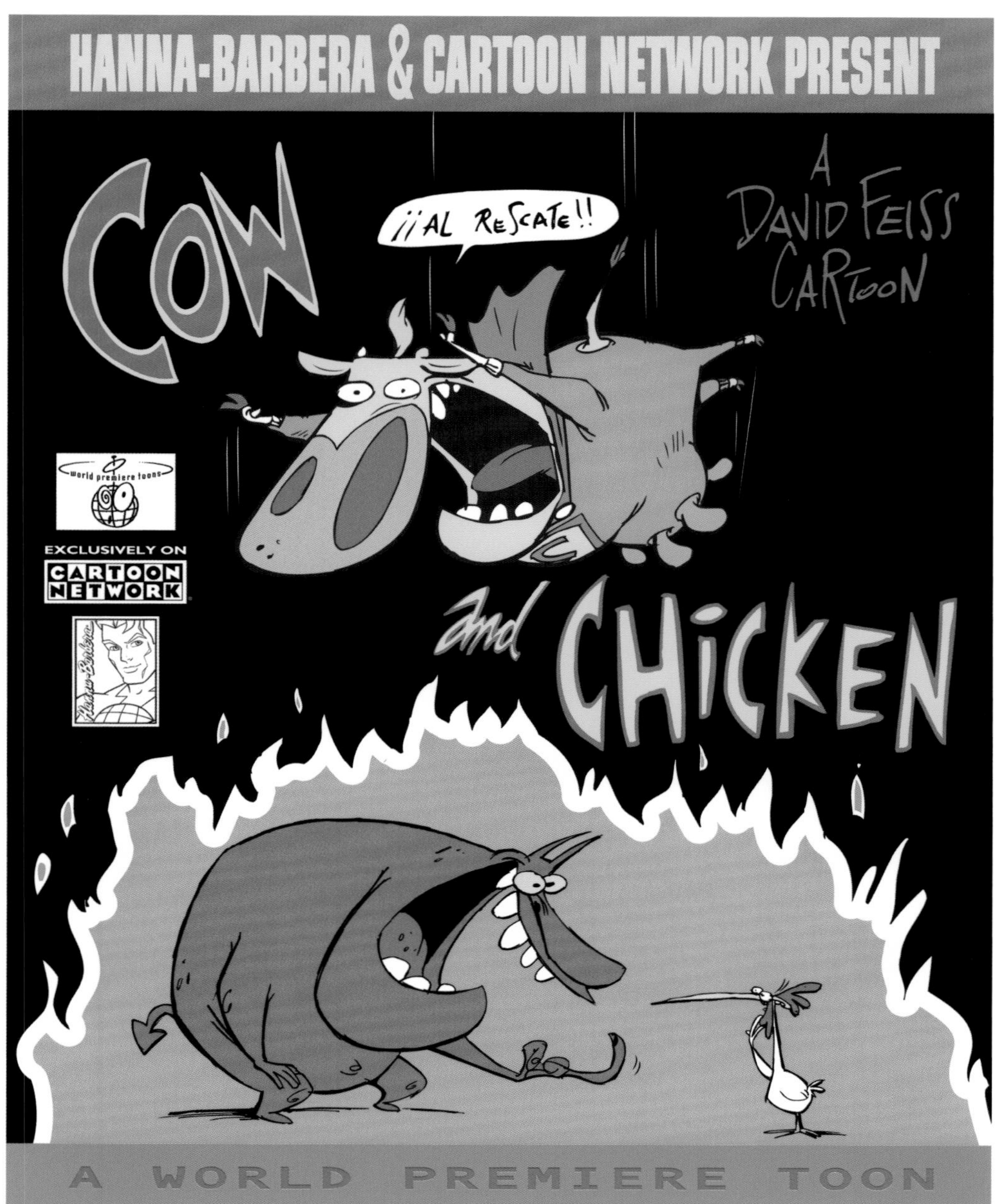

Cow & Chicken created by David Feiss
Art direction and design by Jesse Stagg & Kelly Wheeler

Dexter's Laboratory created by Genndy Tartakovsky
Art direction and design by Jesse Stagg & Kelly Wheeler

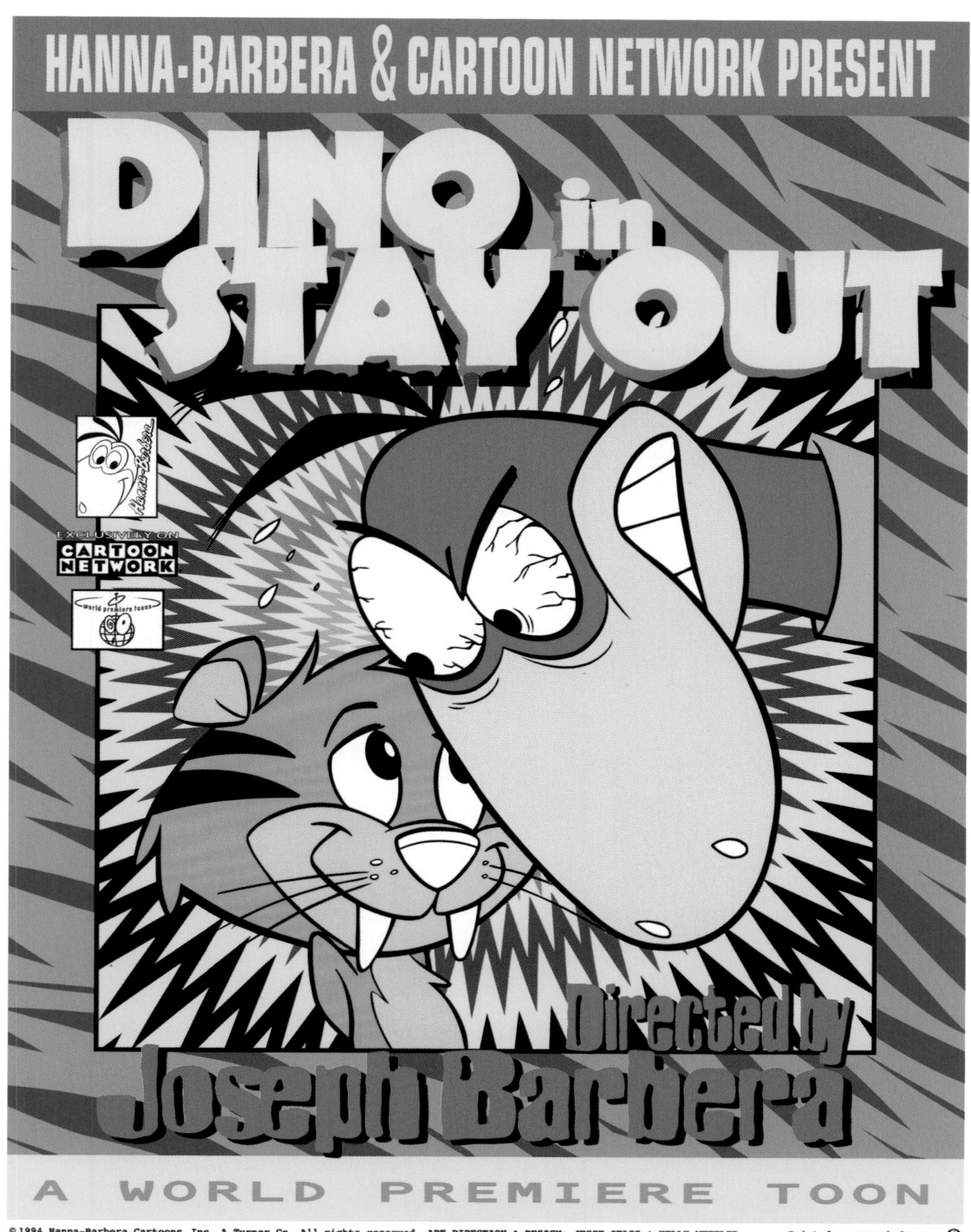

Directed by Joseph Barbera
Art direction and design by Jesse Stagg & Kelly Wheeler

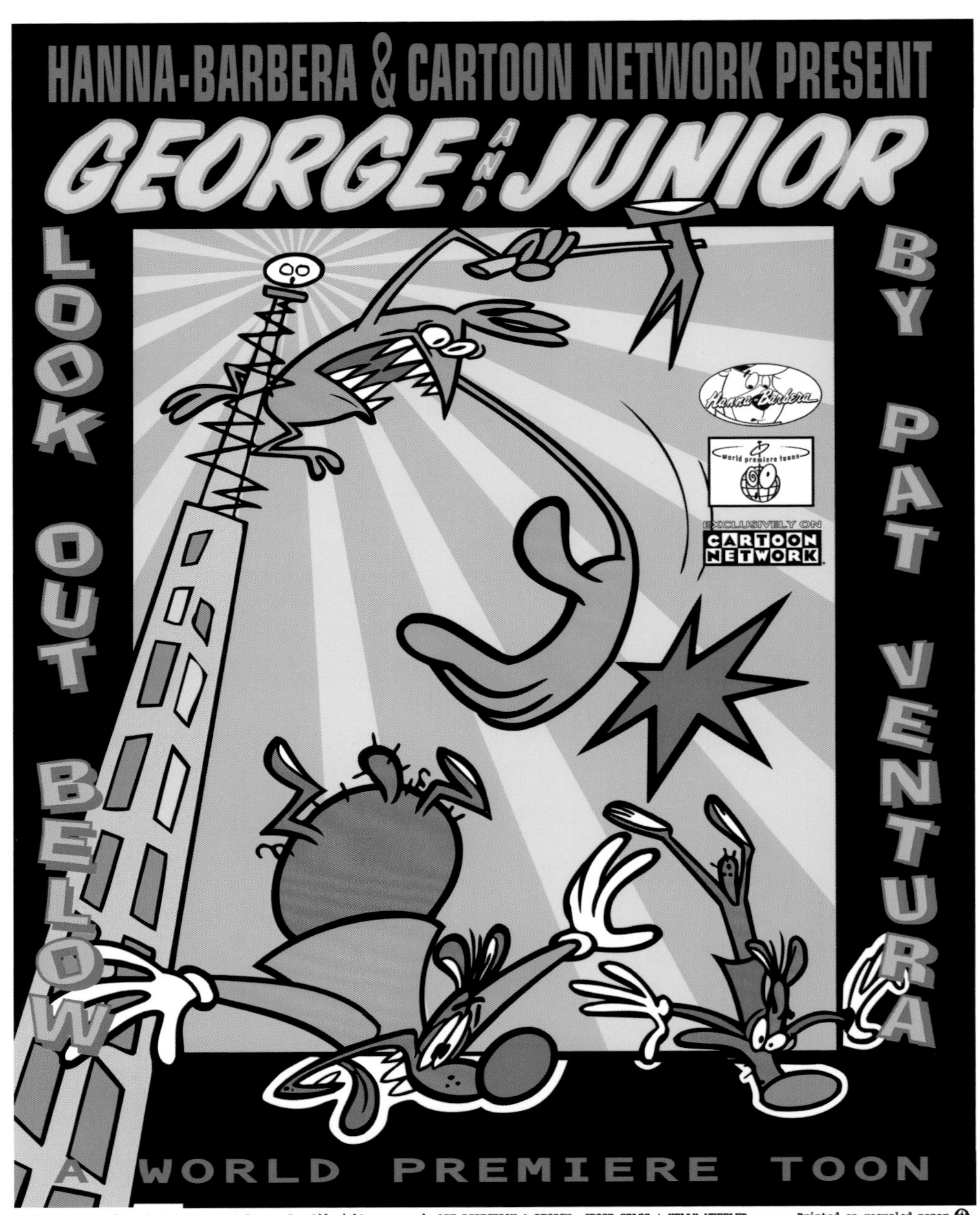

George and Junior created by 'Pat' Ventura
Art direction and design by Jesse Stagg & Kelly Wheeler

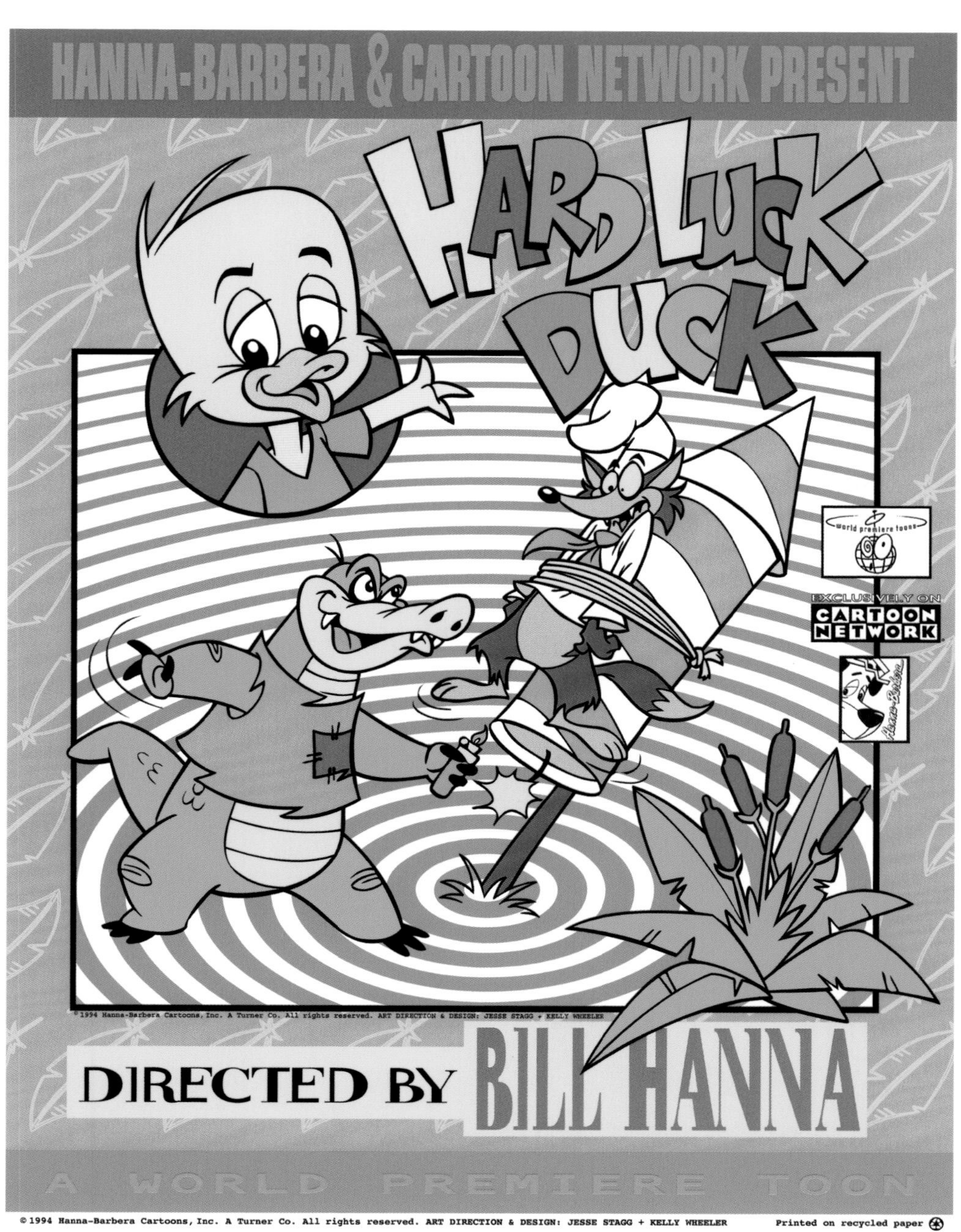

Hard Luck Duck created by Bill Hanna
Art direction and design by Jesse Stagg & Kelly Wheeler

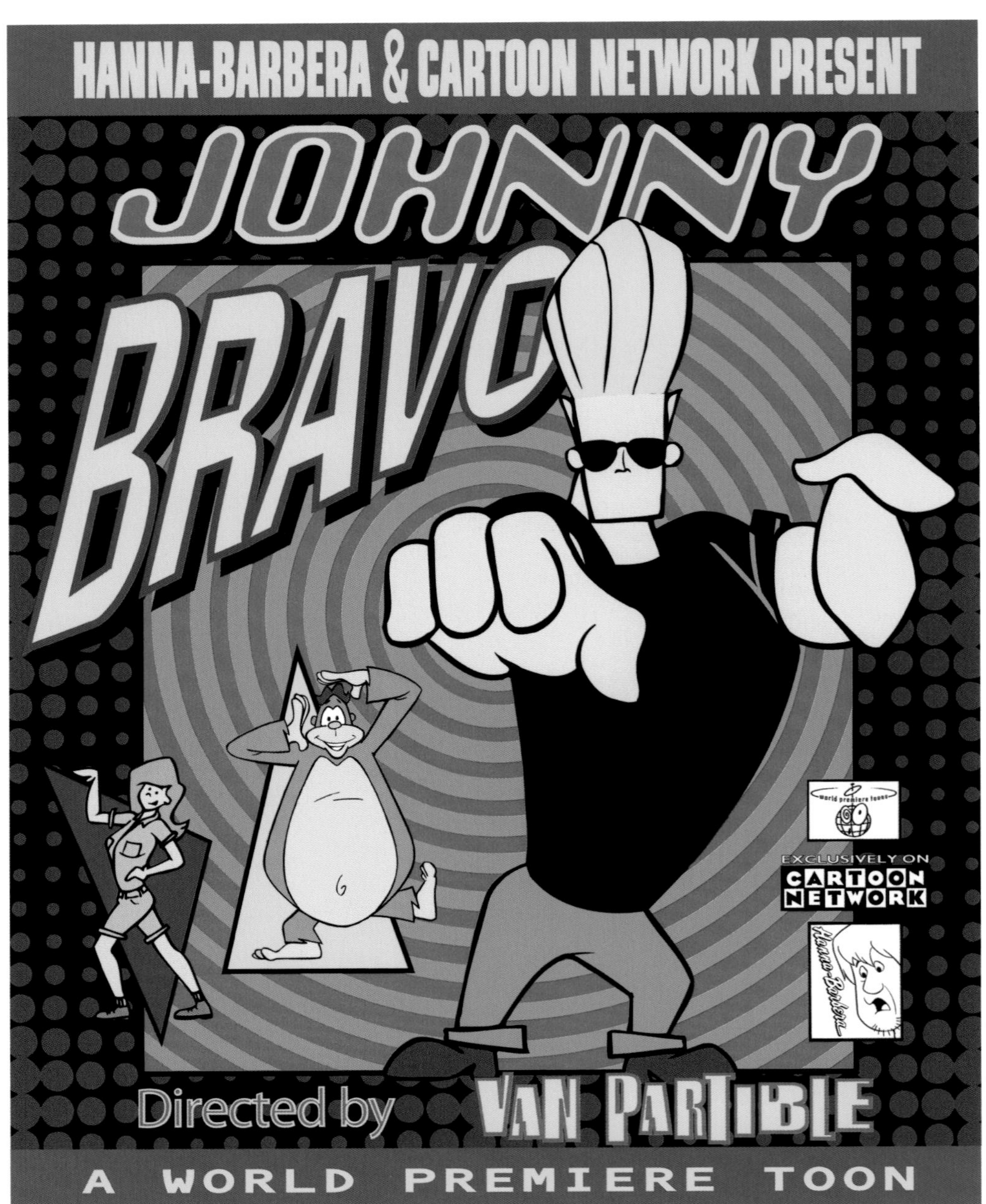

Johnny Bravo created by Van Partible
Art direction and design by Jesse Stagg & Kelly Wheeler

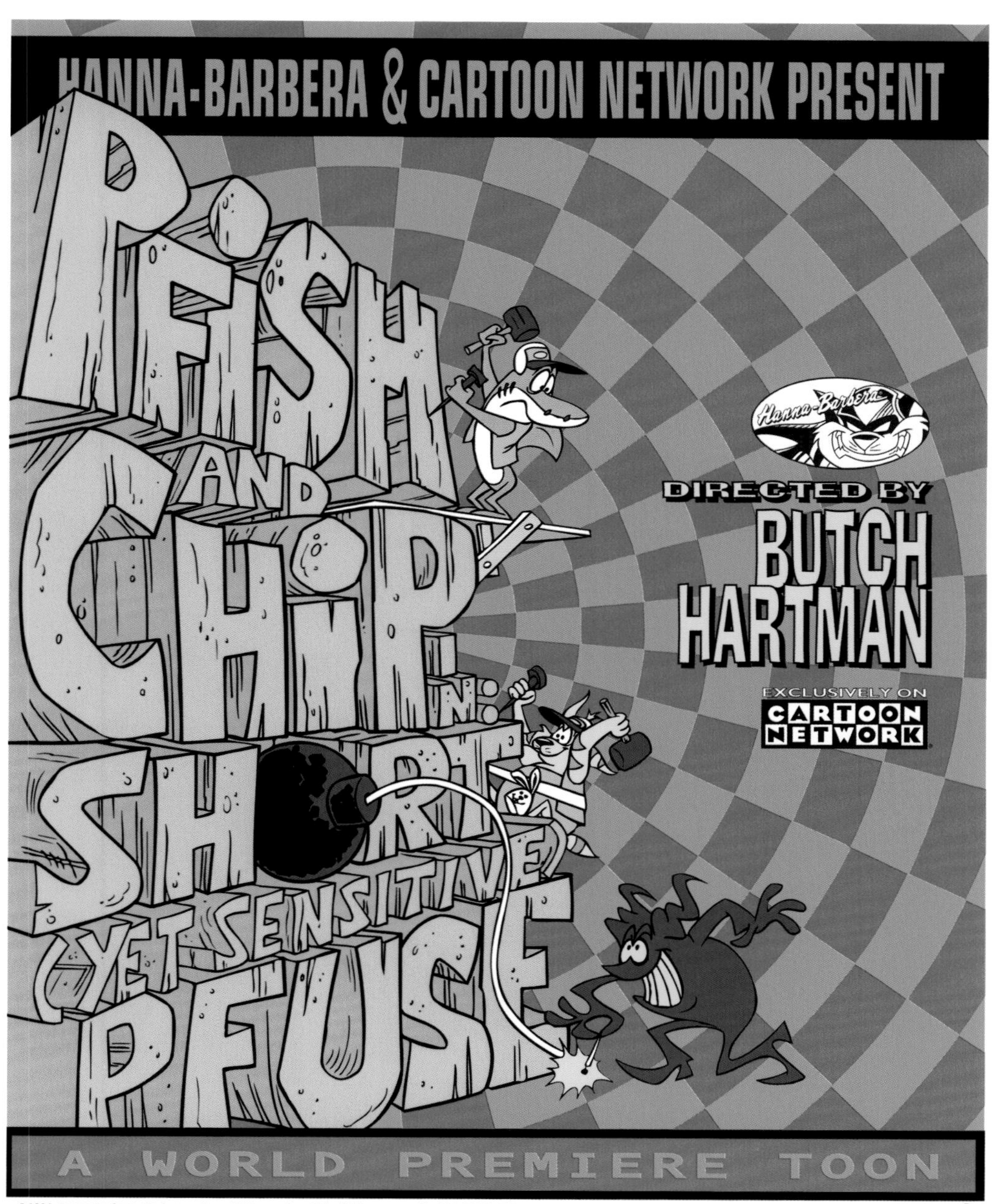

Pfish and Chip created by Butch Hartman,
Eugene Mattos & Michael Raan
Art direction and design by Jesse Stagg & Kelly Wheeler

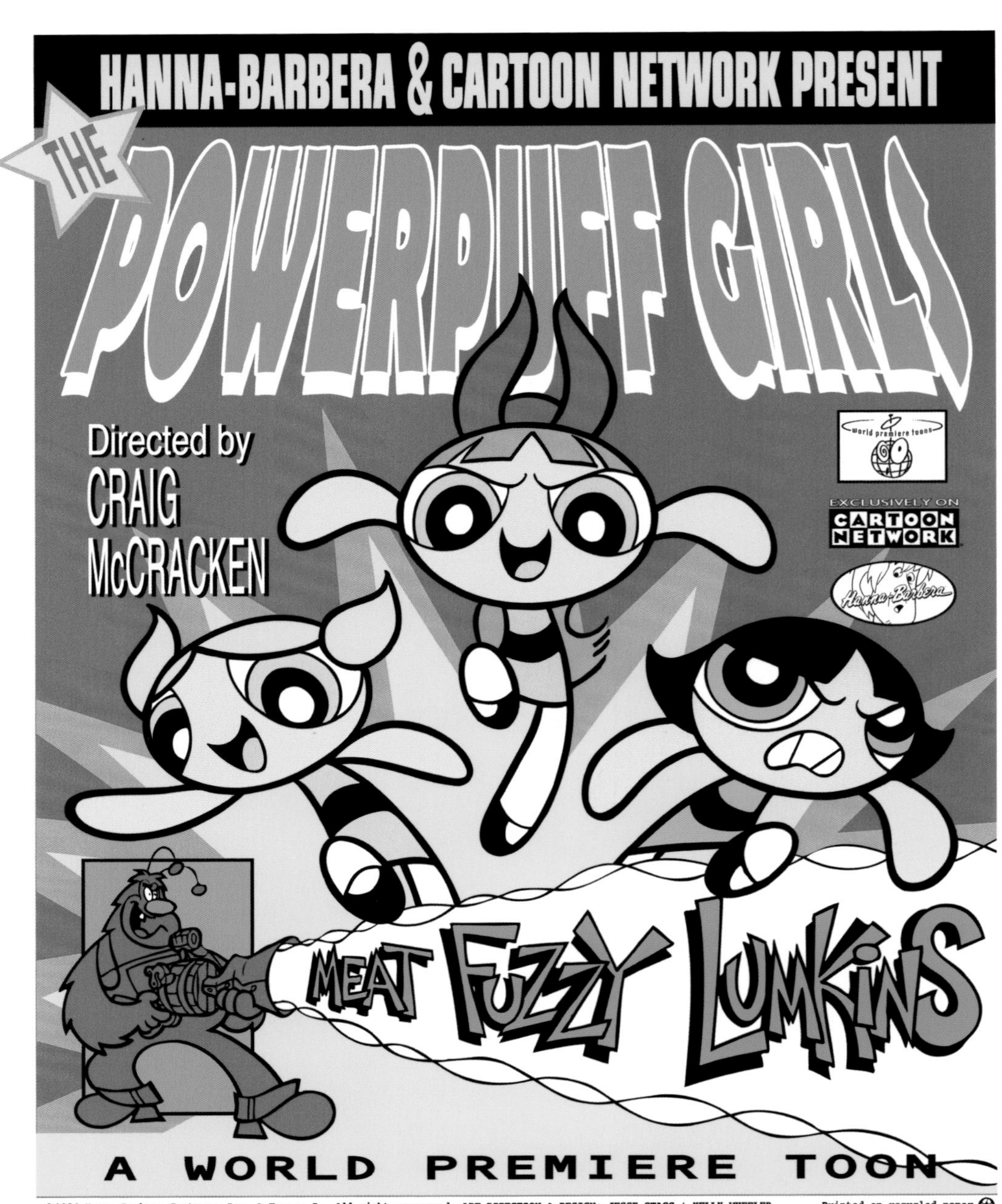

Powerpuff Girls created by Craig McCracken
Art direction and design by Jesse Stagg & Kelly Wheeler

The Worm created by Eddie Fitzgerald
Art direction and design by Jesse Stagg & Kelly Wheeler

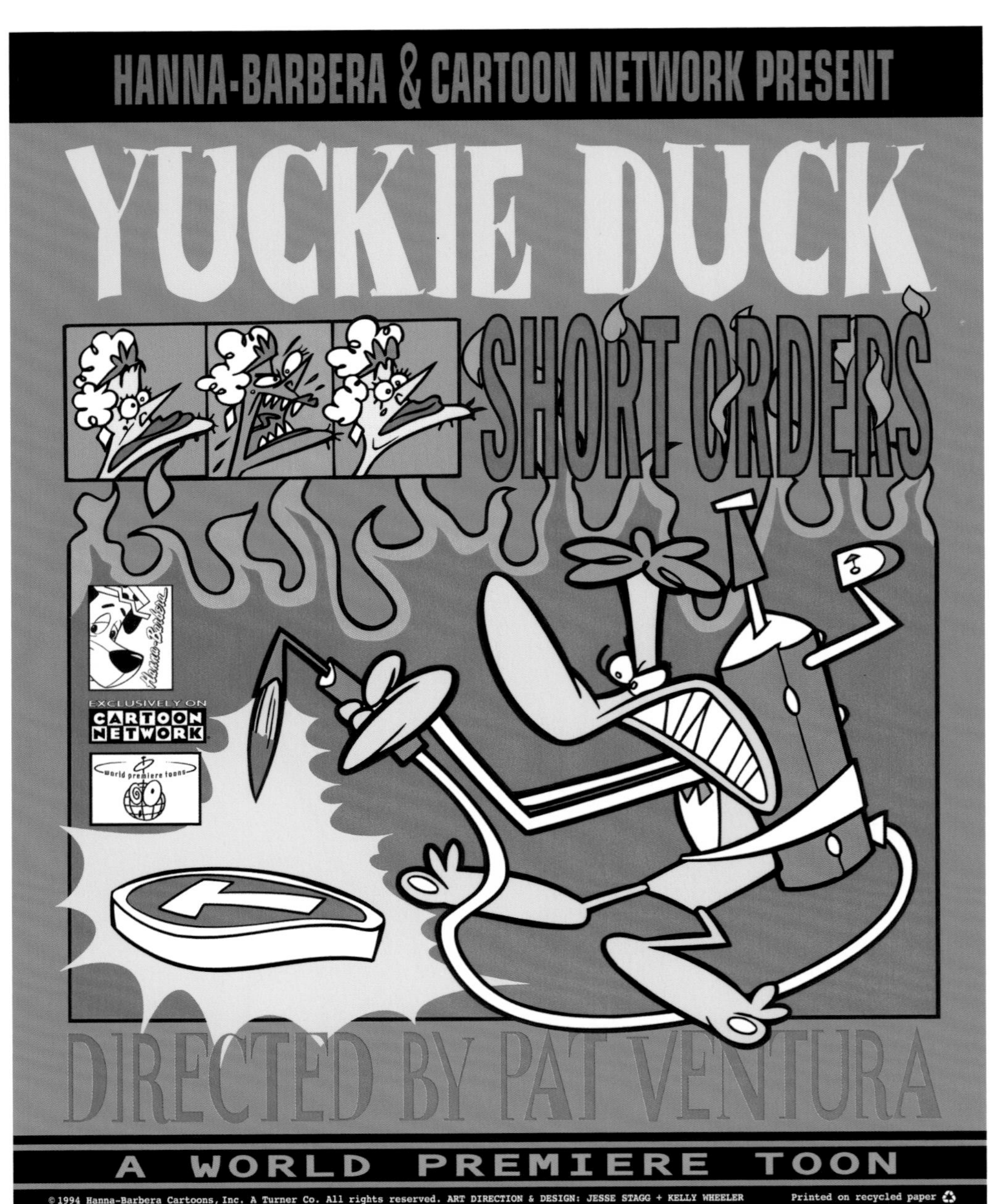

Yucky Duck created by 'Pat' Ventura
Art direction and design by Jesse Stagg & Kelly Wheeler

ChalkZone created by Bill Burnett & Larry Huber
Painting by Frank Rocco

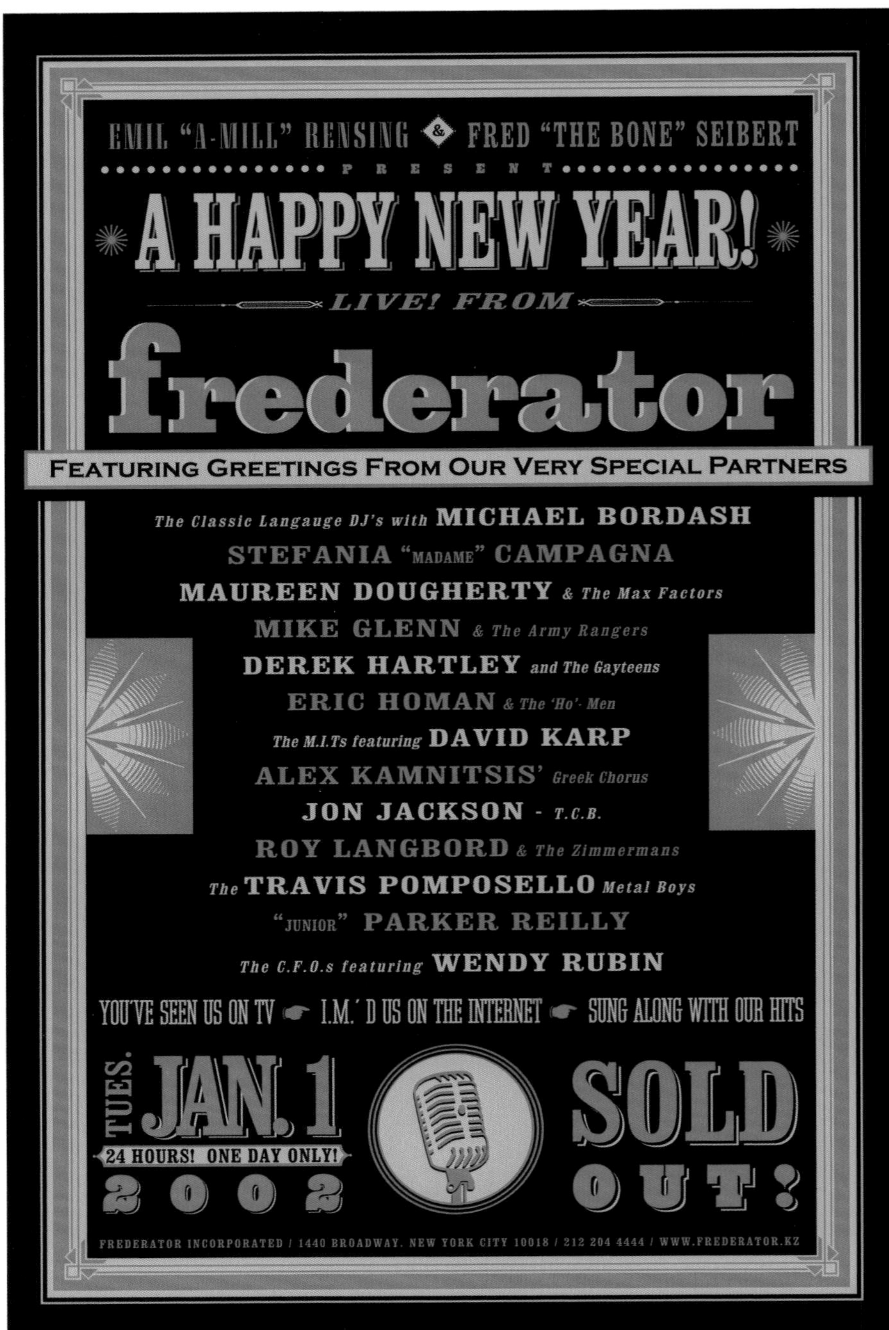

Designed by Patrick Raske

Designed by Jorge R. Gutierrez

HAPPY NEW YEAR!

2004

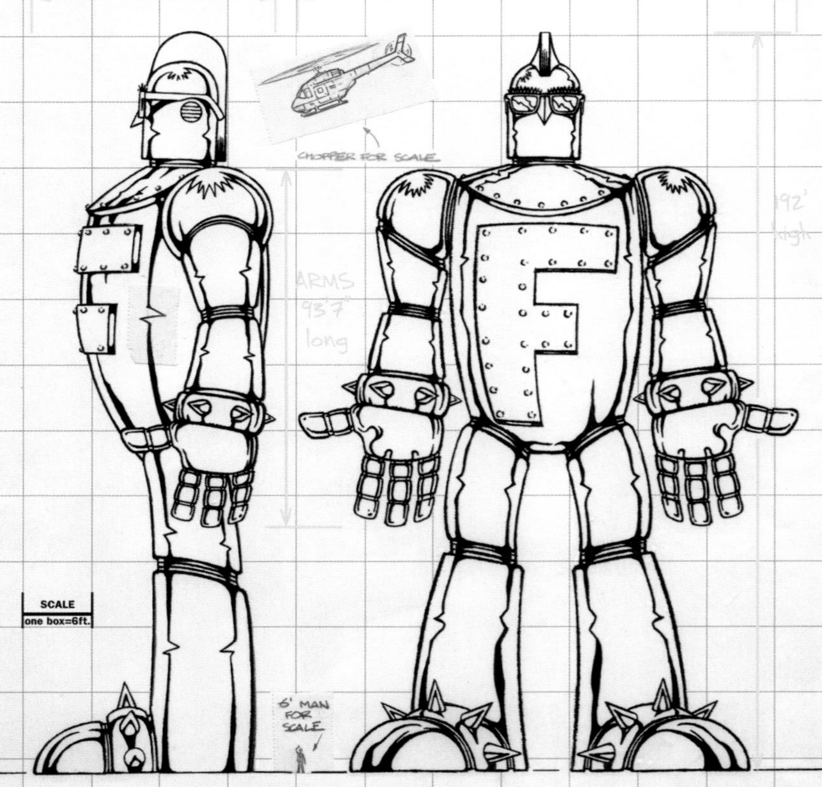

FREDERATOR STUDIOS

ORIGINAL CARTOONS SINCE 1998

www.Frederator.kz · 253 Fifth Avenue. NY, NY 10016 · 231 West Olive Avenue, Burbank, California 91502

The Instigator

By Steven Heller

Fred Seibert's career proves that it is not necessary to be a Yale/Cranbrook/RISD/SVA educated, AIGA/TypeDirectors/Art Director's Club-award-winning, bona fide/pedigreed/certified graphic designer, or any other kind of designer, to create the most indelible visual identities for some of the most visible pop culture media in the world. You just have to be a fan. A fervent, ardent, passionate devotee of "people who do fantastic work in music and visual stuff," as Seibert puts it.

Oh, yeah, you also have to have the vision thing.

Without vision, and the talent, know-how and ambition to realize it, Seibert might have become a tie-dyed-in-the-wool Dead Head selling pot brownies from the back of a psychedelicized microbus. Instead, he instigated, orchestrated, facilitated and otherwise dreamed-up the nascent visual personas of MTV and Nickelodeon, back when they were truly vanguards of the pop-cultural revolution. In the ensuing years he has exerted a significant influence on the look and content of animated cartoons, first as president of Hanna-Barbera and later as the founder of Frederator, a cartoon production company that provides programming to the Cartoon Network. If these accomplishments were not enough for one lifetime, he has recently become president of both MTV Networks Online and Nickelodeon Online, where he has had a hand in transforming the Internet by provoking, stimulating and triggering numerous creative collisions.

"Seibert may not fit the accepted definition of a graphic designer, but he practices design in the emerging sense of the term, as a producer of ideas," says Forrest Richardson, a graphic designer and a member of the 1999 AIGA Medal selection committee. "Seibert designs in the broadest sense by enlisting other people who create unprecedented ideas. Just look at what he has spawned."

What he spawned was a series of environments – at MTV, Nickelodeon, Hanna-Barbera and the Cartoon Network – where creative misfits were able to create unconventional film and animation that otherwise would have had few, if any, outlets. And possessed with a keen ability to see beyond the current thing to the next big thing, and even a few things beyond that, Seibert has a knack for predicting what the public will like, because as a fan he likes it too. In a formal sense, he constructs complex matrices of interconnected concepts designed to support overarching visual communications that project mnemonic identifying images. More simply put, he matches the right person with the best project to get extraordinary results. Moreover, he understands the distinction between integration and interference and rarely asks creative people to slavishly execute his own ideas. "They will do it grudgingly, and expensively," he explains. Rather, he defines contexts, provides opportunities and encourages individual points of view that are used as components of larger programs. He employs those people – young and old, neophyte and veteran – who can interpret a basic blueprint and transcend its confines. So in addition to being an ersatz designer, Seibert is a full-blown impresario. He is also the proverbial whiz kid, the one who always dreamed of making great things.

"The Beatles proved that you could zig and zag through various polarities and still be the thing that you were," recalls Seibert, who was born in 1951 and heard the Beatles for the first time when he was 12 years old. He still speaks of that defining moment with breathless enthusiasm. "It was a really inspiring thing for me to know that you could go from Sergeant Pepper's to the White Album, from 'I Want To Hold Your Hand' to 'A Day In The Life,' from Rubber Soul to Let It Be. I also found inspiration in the fact that they were the ultimate 20th century media thing. They wanted to be a beast of the media and appeal to millions and millions and millions of people, and make trillions and trillions and trillions of dollars, but they did not think that that was in any way counter to making art."

Seibert always wanted to be in the music business. In his

early 20s he had a brief stint as a DJ on a college radio station and later produced avant-garde jazz records for a small independent label. Yet he failed to attain his goal of pop record producer because, he laments, "I didn't smoke enough dope." At 27, he stumbled into the promotion side of the radio business and was hired by adman Dale Pon, who introduced him to Bob Pittman. Pittman was a 25-year-old radio programmer who had just switched over to the cable TV business to shepherd a new venture: a channel that would show music videos 24 hours a day. Pittman invited Seibert to join him in the venture that would become MTV, and with trepidation he complied. "I watched television, I didn't make it," Seibert says about his initial misgivings. And yet all those hours spent in front of the tube had left him with a natural affinity for the medium.

The cable business was so new that virtually anything Seibert tried earned praise. One of his first promos was a kinetic montage of images cut to the beat of claps in the song, "Car Wash." "They [the bigwigs] thought it was an amazing thing," he reports. "I guess television didn't usually do things to the beat." Virtually unfettered Seibert continued to intuitively brand the emerging channel through quirky spots and bumpers. "In those days we didn't know the word 'brand,' and so we broke many of the rules that had governed television's identity for decades," he remembers. Seibert, with his friend and MTV colleague Alan

Goodman, used cable TV as a laboratory for a slew of unprecedented animations. The idea was to entertain rather than push sales pitches down the audience's throats. And in the process, Seibert wanted to unleash the talents of creative people he had always admired.

As a teen, Seibert was inspired by the wellspring of innovative graphic design and packaging that came out of Columbia Records during the '60s and early '70s. He particularly admired the work of art director John Berg who, he explains, "created a language that reflected the wildly diverse sensibilities of type design, photographic imagery and portraiture of the time. And yet there was this amazing consistency, a quality of ideas that went through the whole thing." (Inspired by this work, Seibert taught himself to "design" covers for his own company, Oblivion Records, which he founded while working at MTV.) When he launched the promotions for MTV, his model was not Lou Dorfsman's legendary advertising for CBS Television, which was considered the industry standard, but Berg's art direction for Columbia. "I wanted the MTV visuals to be like album covers for television," he says. Seibert began his work at MTV with the idea that since music was multifaceted, the network should avoid projecting a rigid corporate persona or, for that matter, anything corporate looking. The television industry revered the sanctity of logos: the CBS Eye (1951), NBC Peacock (1956) and ABC circle (1961) embodied the networks' respective ethos and were thus immutable and inviolable. So Seibert's first instinct was to avoid the I.D. firms that churned out the most expensive corporate identity systems. Instead, he commissioned a childhood friend, Frank Olinsky, who was a principal along with Pat Gorman and Patti Rogoff in Manhattan Design, a very small graphics and illustration office tucked behind a tai chi studio in Manhattan's Greenwich Village. Although they had no previous corporate identity experience, Seibert chose them "because I'd been friends with Frank since I was four years old, and he was talented even then." He also loved rock and roll. Luckily, Bob Pittman agreed that the logo could take any form as long as the "call letters" were readable.

The first version of the "M" was inspired when Patti Rogoff walked past a graffiti-scrawled schoolyard wall. At that moment she realized MTV's logo had to be made of three-dimensional letters that exuded street culture. After many false starts, Pat Gorman finessed a large M and hand-scrawled a little "TV" onto it, which Olinsky thought was ugly. He argued that if the concept was going to work, a better rendering of "TV" was imperative. But their real breakthrough came when Gorman and Olinsky decided that the M could be something like a screen on which various images could be "projected." And the M could become an object – a birthday cake, or a bologna sandwich or whatever else they wanted to make it. The shape of the M could be transformed into anything, as long as it continued to look like an M. Back at headquarters, MTV executives were troubled by the solution. They felt that the M was not legible. And their lawyers argued that a mutable logo would require repeated registration each time a different iteration was used. Seibert, however, was not concerned. Five variations of the logo were pinned up on his wall for weeks because he couldn't make up his mind which one he liked best. Finally, he decided it would be "very rock and roll" to use them all in animated sequences. It seemed like the problem was solved.

Still, the head of sales lobbied to kill the logo because he didn't want to send such a flagrantly unconventional design to potential advertising buyers. Seibert recalls that he was asked by the muckety-mucks if he really thought that this logo would last as long as the CBS Eye. His answer was a resounding "No." "Why would I think that a rock thing would stand up to the icon of TV logos?" The executives insisted that Seibert approach some "real" designers, including Push Pin Studios and Lou Dorfsman, which he did. But Seibert kept total faith in the original idea and slyly admits, "I sandbagged the assignment. They all did terrible work and then we were out of time." So with a small type variation on the "Music Television" subtitle, the original was approved a few weeks before the new channel went on the air, on August 1, 1981.

The televised MTV logo was the perfect embodiment both of raucous rock and roll and of MTV's promise to change forever ordinary viewing (and listening) habits. Its animated mutability made it as anticipated a feature of daily programming as the music videos themselves. Over time various illustrators were hired, including John van Hammersveld, Mark Marek, Lynda Barry and Steven Guarnaccia, to transform the basic prop into mini-metaphors. But the most important vehicle for establishing the logo's supremacy were 25 10-second animated spots in which the logo changed design and meaning. This included the most recurring and iconic spot, an appropriation of the famous photograph of the first man landing on moon with a vibrating, ever-changing MTV logo used in place of the American flag. "Ultimately," recalls Seibert, "we did three or four hundred promos that were the real heartbeat of the 'newness' of MTV."

Four years after MTV launched, Seibert and Alan Goodman helped restructure a floundering Nickelodeon, transforming it from a repository of stale cartoons to a content-driven destination of original entertainment for young and old. Unlike network TV, where programming aims for high ratings at all costs (by filling the air with trendy action heroes or "When Pets Attack"), Nickelodeon was determined to do things right, with stories and characters that were good from a kid's point of view. "If we did that well, then we'd make money," says Seibert. Within a year, the channel's ratings had made a huge jump. The duo also devised Nick-at-Nite, a brilliant scheme to broadcast reruns of baby-boom TV classics during the time slots when younger kids were in bed. For Seibert this was more than a retrogimmick, it was a move to philosophically position the channel as a repository of great pop culture. "Back then, old television was considered even more disposable than old music," he explains, "and I was determined to prove–even to Gerry Laybourne who ran Nickelodeon–that it wasn't junk, that it has cultural value."

Which is the reason why after leaving MTV and Nickelodeon he accepted the top job at Hanna-Barbera, the cartoon studio known for its pioneering "limited animation" style, yet which for decades had been churning out mediocre reprises of their cartoon classics, which included "The Flintstones," "The Jetsons," "Yogi Bear," and others. Seibert understood that with the success of Matt Groening's "The Simpsons" and John Kricfalusi's "Ren and Stimpy," a new generation of cartoon creators was waiting to be tapped. He immediately altered the archaic internal organization of Hanna-Barbera, which emphasized production over concept and technicians over artists. His model was based on creative teams that enabled new ideas to take precedence over old chestnuts. He soon oversaw the creation of HB's first new series in decades, "Two Stupid Dogs." The cartoon did not do well, yet out of this failure he devised a unique concept called "What A Cartoon." Instead of investing a lot of money in one 13-show series, he used the same capital to produce 48 speculative cartoons, each made by one artist and a team of production people. "What A Cartoon" was an anthology of speculations, and the most successful ones were spun-off into series, later produced by Frederator. The successes included such current hits as "Dexter's Laboratory," "The Powerpuff Girls," "Cow and Chicken,"and "Johnny Bravo."

Seibert is a product of 1960s mass media, and he admits to a somewhat schizophrenic relationship with the branding that he has done so well. "I am deeply cynical about the goals of branding, which to me, in its purest form, means higher CPMs [cost-per-thousand] for advertising. But I realize that the values that I am looking to change through the work that I do ultimately give value to advertising. That's the cynical side." The other side of the relationship is more deeply rooted: "I feel like a '60s child, always attracted to things that were disenfranchising to me," he says. And this is what comes through in the music, cartoons and comics he has fervently tried to integrate into today's mainstream. "I was very resentful of the fact that in the '60s people said that the music I liked was 'disposable.' It definitely wasn't disposable to me. So one of the things in the back of my mind in the work I was doing at MTV was, 'I'll make them listen!' and give this stuff new value."

MTV and Nickelodeon are wildly successful today. And given the current reach of cable and satellite TV, their identities may be more recognized internationally than all the networks combined. Irreverent, oddball and sometimes-gross cartoons also fill television now more than ever. Seibert must be given credit for a fair share of this.

Yet Seibert's chronic restlessness prevents him from basking too long in the glow of previous accomplishments. For the past three years he has been working in the newest mass medium, as a player in the Internet. After his stint at Hanna-Barbera, he became president of MTV Networks Online, a position he now holds at Nickelodeon Online. He confides that "I don't have a bottom of my toes feeling yet" about the new media. Yet complete mastery of a medium has never been a handicap for him before. Rather, his unflagging enthusiasm for the creative potential of the medium is what makes him invaluable. "What I do with the Internet is find unbelievably talented people, the way I always have, put them in a room where the best ideas can come out, then defend their right to have ideas and fail or succeed." As a fan, he adds, "I follow these great people and I've found myself attracted to places where great people are attracted. I figured that by the rub-off of their greatness, I could feel better." Seibert's modesty is not false. His exposure to a legion of creative people who have worked for him has definitely enriched his life. But in the final analysis, because Seibert has spent his career instigating creative people, the media, popular culture and the mass audience has been greatly enriched, too.

Steven Heller, art director of the New York Times Book Review, *is the co-chair of the School of Visual Arts MFA/Design program. He is the author of over 90 books on graphic design and popular art, including* Paul Rand *(Phaidon)*, Typology: Type Design from the Victorian Era To the Digital Age *(Chronicle Books)*, Handwritten: Expressive Lettering in the Digital Age *(Thames and Hudson)*, Merz to Emigre and Beyond: Avant Garde Magazine Design of the 20th Century *(Phaidon Press)*. Design Literacy Second Edition, Design Dialogues, The Graphic Design Reader *and* The Swastika: Symbol Beyond Redemption *(Allworth Press)*.

Original Cartoons: The Frederator Studios Postcards 1998-2005

Edited by
Eric Homan & Fred Seibert